AN AUTOCORRELATION
THEORY OF FORM
DETECTION

For Michan
Taneil
Lynet
Lisa

(*My Ladies*)

AN AUTOCORRELATION THEORY OF FORM DETECTION

WILLIAM R. UTTAL
The University of Michigan

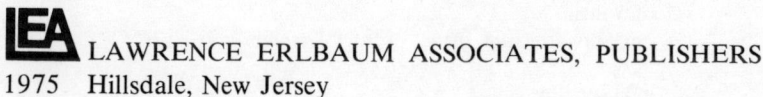 LAWRENCE ERLBAUM ASSOCIATES, PUBLISHERS
1975   Hillsdale, New Jersey

DISTRIBUTED BY THE HALSTED PRESS DIVISION OF
JOHN WILEY & SONS
New York   Toronto   London   Sydney

Copyright © 1975 by Lawrence Erlbaum Associates, Inc.
All rights reserved. No part of this book may be reproduced in any form, by photostat, microform, retrieval system, or any other means, without the prior written permission of the publisher.

Lawrence Erlbaum Associates, Inc., Publishers
62 Maria Drive
Hillsdale, New Jersey 07642

Distributed solely by Halsted Press Division
John Wiley & Sons, Inc., New York

Library of Congress Cataloging in Publication Data

Uttal, William R
   An autocorrelation theory of form detection.

   Bibliography: p.
   Includes indexes.
   1. Form perception.   I. Title.
BF293.U85   153.7'52   75-4911
ISBN 0-470-89654-X

Printed in the United States of America

Contents

Preface vii

1 Theories of Perception 1

    I. Introduction   1
    II. Six Stages of Perception   5
    III. Review of Earlier Theories of Form Detection   10
        A. Sensory–Motor Theories   12
        B. Neurophysiological Theories   13
        C. Computational Network Theories   20
        D. Correlation Theories   23

2 The Psychophysical Experiments 31

    I. General Method of Present Experiments   31
        A. Subjects   31
        B. Apparatus   32
        C. Procedure   34
        D. Unique Attributes of the Dot-Masking Technique   35
        E. Specific Advantages of the Dot-Masking Technique   35
    II. Some Experimental Studies   39
        A. Introduction   39
        B. Experiment I: Effect of Dot Numerosity on Line Detection   40
        C. Experiment II: The Effect of Orientation on Line Detection   43

D. Experiment III: The Effect of Curvature and Angulature on Line Detection 46
E. Experiment IV: The Effect of Irregular Spacing on Collinear Dotted-Line Detection 52
F. Experiment V: The Effect of Transverse Irregular Spacing on Dotted-Line Detection 56
G. Experiment VI: Critical Parts in Triangle Recognition 58
H. Experiment VII: The Effect of Rotation on the Detection of Polygons 62

III. Some Experiments on Organization 65
A. Experiment VIII. The Effect of Figural Organization on Dotted-Form Detection 66
B. Experiment IX: Further Effects of Figural Organization 69
C. Experiment X: Even Further Effects of Figural Organization on Dotted-Form Detection 74
D. Experiment XI: Effect of Ordered Figural Goodness on Dotted-Form Detection 78
E. Experiment XII: The Locus of the Dot-Masking Phenomenon 81

3 The Theory 89

I. A Summary of the Experimental Findings 89
II. Basic Properties of the Autocorrelation Model 93
III. A Computer Simulation of the Autocorrelation Model 96
IV. Theory of the Model 98
V. Tests of the Model 103
VI. Speculations on a Neurophysiological Autocorrelator 126

4 Summary—An Alternative Neural Implementation 131

References 142

Author Index 151
Subject Index 154

Preface

The goal of the research described in this study is the understanding of how the organization of stimulus patterns affects visual perception. This topic has been deemphasized in recent years as the inadequacies of earlier Gestalt theories became apparent. However, the Gestalt *descriptions* of visual processes still ring true, despite the fact that their *theories* have been supplanted. These descriptions suggest that the human perceiver operates on global factors of stimuli rather than on the details of their component features. Yet much recent research, it seems, has been focused on the analysis of figures into parts rather than on considerations of overall organization, in spite of the fact that people seem to do just the opposite. This focus has, in large part, been stimulated by important developments in computer technology and neurophysiology, but, unfortunately, seems to ignore the psychological findings.

In the chapters to follow, I spell out the results of an experimental program and a simulation model that concentrates on a theory which emphasizes the organization of forms rather than the parts of which they are made. In this regard, at once, I return to a perspective championed by Gestalt psychologists decades ago and move ahead from feature to organization in a modern experimental context.

Human form perception is so complex and involves such a variety of distinguishable processes that it would be entirely inappropriate to suggest that a general theory will soon be forthcoming. In the contemporary context, any progress to be made must be based instead on an intentional abstraction of some lesser part, from the entire process of perception, for detailed examination. To do this requires that an experimental paradigm be utilized that is sensitive to the particular aspects under investigation. Dots and patterns of dots are the experimental vehicle of choice in this study. Dot patterns have a number of advantages but the main one is that the characteristics of geometric organization are emphasized rather than the characteristics of the component features of a stimulus.

Although this report reflects a personal viewpoint, it is one that has grown out of the interactions that I have had with a number of colleagues. Most important has been the specific suggestion by Dodwell (1971) that the data obtained in my laboratory may be explicable with some sort of an autocorrelation model. The idea has grown and been nurtured by interactions with my associates at The University of Michigan. I am specifically indebted to my colleagues James O. Chinnis, Jr., Larry Goble, and Joseph Mesrich, who have stimulated the growth of the ideas presented in this paper in many different ways. Consultation with Walter Reitman, Daniel Green, and Robert Lindsay has helped to clarify some of the ideas embodied in the neural model. Tadasu Oyama (of Chiba University in Japan) read the entire manuscript and made several helpful suggestions concerning the structure of the discussion.

I am also extremely grateful to the following people who have helped in the progress of this study: Ms. Lynn Gore and Ms. Thelma Eskin have been indefatigable and always highly organized in their supervision of laboratory operations, in preparation of stimuli, in data analysis, and in typing and editing the manuscript. After we did all that we could with manuscripts, we turned to Ms. Claire Adler, a "super" editor, to help polish the final version. Her contributions to the clarity of this document are deeply appreciated. Ms. Judy Fitzgerald programmed the simulation model of the autocorrelator and produced the many autocorrelations necessary for our discussion, as well as wrote the experimental control program. The contribution of Ms. Kathie Gourlay who initially modified the Williamson (1972) algorithm for perspective drawings of three-dimensional plots is also gratefully acknowledged.

Part of this book was written during the summer of 1973 while I was a guest of the Laboratory of Sensory Sciences at the University of Hawaii. I am most happy to express my appreciation to the trio of directors of the Laboratory, Drs. M. E. Bitterman, Robert Cole, and Ian Cooke, for their hospitality during that fine summer.

All of the work here has been supported both by The University of Michigan and by grants from the Federal Government. I am grateful for support over the years from the Mental Health Research Institute and from the National Science Foundation and the National Institutes of Mental Health. I am especially appreciative of an NIMH Research Scientist Award, the result of a particular enlightened policy that has helped a number of scientists to do some things that otherwise might not have been possible.

As always, whatever I accomplish is in large part due to my dear wife and my three little girls who are in the process of becoming three fine women.

WILLIAM R. UTTAL
Ann Arbor, Michigan

1
Theories of Perception

I. INTRODUCTION

How do people visually recognize forms or patterns? This question has been of persistent interest to philosophers and psychologists for hundreds of years. From time to time, explanations have been proposed based on principles varying from vaguely qualitative descriptions to highly specific analogies with contemporary neurophysiological findings or computer architecture. In spite of this continued interest in the problem, there is as yet little agreement among workers in the field on specific answers to even the simplest questions. For example, it still is not known what enables us to see straight lines, or even if such a stimulus is indeed perceptually "simpler" than a more complex form. A major reason for this lack of consensus is that over the years little research has dealt directly with the problem of form perception in a manner that is directly relevant to the most important issues. Research has been directed mainly at secondary aspects of the question, such as discrimination between forms, adaptation to distorted forms, or the temporal interactions between portions of forms, rather than at those aspects of pattern organization which are more likely the primary stimulus determinants of form recognition. Attneave and Arnoult (1956) made this point when they said "there is virtually no psychophysics of shape or pattern." This deficiency has been summed up recently best, perhaps, by Zusne (1970), who notes, speaking of the continuing difficulty of computerizing (i.e., modeling) the pattern recognition process:

> . . . the problem of pattern recognition has not yet been solved on the psychological level. The physical dimensions of form that determine recognition and the range of their variability have not been specified yet.

Sutherland (1967), considering the contents of an important pattern recognition symposium (Wathen-Dunn, 1967), has likewise noted that most of the papers have dealt with the labeling act or the time constants of visual perception, rather than with the primary question of "which features of the pattern are used in the classification process."

There are obvious reasons for this paucity of relevant data. At best, form recognition is an ill-defined area of study. Few workers have even explicitly defined a "form." Furthermore, the tasks used as measures of recognition performance may vary from the simplest detection task to some of the most complex responses studied in cognitive psychology. This variation in procedure sometimes leads to the inadvertent mixing of quite different processes under the same rubric.

In this discussion, the words "form" and its near synonym, "pattern," are specifically intended to denote the arrangement or order of a set of components. The nature of the components may vary considerably from one equivalent pattern to another, but the essence of the pattern concept is the global, or overall, structure imposed on parts that may themselves convey no meaning. The term "random pattern" is a *non sequitur*. Patterns are defined by virtue of their order; an unordered, random structure is unpatterned in the most basic sense of the word.

However precise the definition of a pattern may become, what people "do" with patterns in the process of perceiving them is going to remain a separate and complex question. The present study attempts to spell out one approach to answering this question. If there is any single theme in this study, it is that the parts of a stimulus, whatever they may be, are of less importance than the arrangement of those parts. Perhaps nowhere is this point made more effectively than in the fascinating drawings shown in Figure 1-1. This picture is presented by Kolers (1970) in an effort to make a crucial point concerning human visual pattern recognition, namely, that we tend to perceive and categorize visual stimuli more on the basis of the arrangement of the parts than by the nature of the parts. Kolers refers to these patterns as "random forms" and, indeed, if one inspects the various angles, curves, and lines that make up the various forms, it is true that they do exhibit a wonderful randomness. However, the arrangement of these parts is not random. It is highly specific and there is no hesitation on the part of the observer to immediately categorize all of these global forms into a single classification. All of the stimulus forms are responded to with a single class name. Furthermore, there is no reason to expect that any other aspect of the response, such as reaction time, varies as a function of the kinds of parts used in the construction of each object.

Our attention is thus directed by Kolers to arrangement and form, in the classical Gestalt sense of the terms, as highly important—and probably critical—attributes in specifying the determining features of the pattern that Zusne and Sutherland feel are so lacking in modern theories of pattern recognition. Once this premise has been accepted, the experimenter faces the problem of the enormous complexity of visual stimuli. To analyze such a problem successfully, it is often advantageous to operate in a context and with a paradigm that helps to isolate the various involved factors. In the following study, a simple stimulus type—patterns of dots—is employed in the expectation that specific parameters can be manipulated such that the dimensions that are critical to recognition can be identified and their individual effects determined. If this is to be done, it is clear that a much simpler process, abstracted from the more complete pattern recognition process,

FIGURE 1-1 A collection of "random" forms composed of a wide variety of specific features or parts. (From Kolers, 1970.)

must be studied. The next section of this study seeks to identify exactly what it is that is being assayed in the present series of experiments and the derived theoretical model.

II. SIX STAGES OF PERCEPTION

When a simple experimental stimulus paradigm such as a pattern of dots is used, the general problem of pattern recognition is simplified. A narrowly defined recognition process that is particularly amenable to parametric manipulation is extracted from the total process. To assist in understanding the meaning of this analysis, the form recognition problem may be considered to be a series of sequential perceptual stages, each of which can be isolated to some degree by the use of a relevant psychophysical instrument. Although this separation into a series of subprocesses cannot be done a priori, examination of contemporary experimental literature suggests that a multiple-stage information-processing system is operating in human vision. A number of authors have suggested various multilevel models of visual perception (see, for example, Turvey, 1973).

Figure 1-2 is a block diagram showing another possible multistage model of the sequence of processes involved in visual form recognition. Here, each stage of information processing can be assumed to set boundary conditions for the succeeding stages; but once the properties of the stimulus pattern exceed the thresholds of any of the preceding boundary conditions, it must be assumed that the contribution of the earlier stages to visual perception is no longer of major consequence. Specifically, this model assumes that there are at least six separable, sequential stages in the visual processing of patterned information.

Stage 1. Stage 1 is concerned mainly with the transduction process and is therefore closely related to the actual physical energetics of the stimulus. It is generally assumed that luminous, chromatic, and acuity thresholds typical of this stage are controlled by neural mechanisms located in the most peripheral elements of the receptor mechanisms. For example, two lights must be of a certain intensity, of a certain color, and sufficiently spaced in order to be discriminated

1. THEORIES OF PERCEPTION

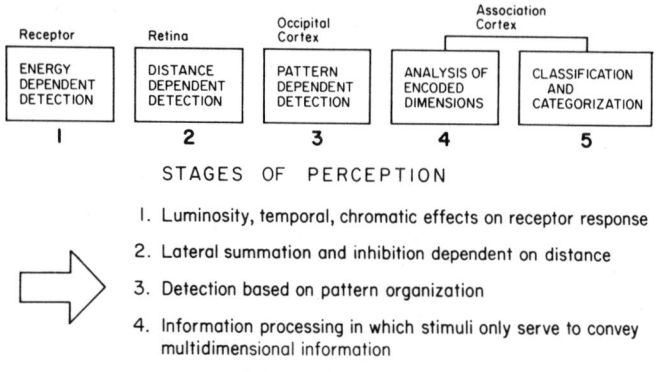

FIGURE 1-2 The five stages of perception. This diagram indicates the parameters critical to each stage, the tasks characteristic of each, and some speculations about the neural levels at which each may occur. The arrow indicates the level of interest in the present study.

as two rather than one (or none). However, except for some modest spatial summation, little about the form of the stimulus is critical to the detection of its presence or absence; most of the characteristics of Stage 1 processing are defined by simple energy considerations. When dot patterns are used to study spatial interaction at this stage, the interactions are very small. For example, Kristofferson (1957) and Kristofferson & Dember (1958) used multiple-dot patterns to study luminosity detection thresholds, clearly a Stage 1 process, and showed that multiple dots raise detection levels above probability summation levels only when interdot distances are less than 10′ of visual angle. This is probably a good estimate of the highly restricted range of simple lateral interactions between small dots and is also in accord with the findings reported by von Békésy (1968).

Stage 2. Stage 2 processes concern interactions between stimuli that are sufficiently above the absolute energetic thresholds to be easily detected when presented alone but that may be suppressed or enhanced as a result of interaction effects between neighboring portions of the retina. Perceptual contour enhancement effects, such as the Mach band or the Hermann grid, are probably the clearest behavioral results of this sort of spatial interaction. Such phenomena are probably mediated by lateral connections in the inner and outer plexiform layers of the retina. To observe these effects, however, the boundary conditions determined by the luminosity thresholds must have been sufficiently exceeded so that they are no longer of consequence. In many of the phenomena at this stage of processing, the geometrical relationships among the stimuli are very important. For example, the spacing between the squares of the Hermann grid, the slope of the gradient in the prototypical Mach band stimulus (see Ratliff, 1965), and related variables are critical in defining the extent and magnitude of the resulting perceptions. When spots of light are larger than small dots, Stage 2 processes become significant.

Stage 3. Stage 3 is also heavily dependent on the specific geometry of the stimulus pattern, but it is assayed by experimental techniques that often involve signal extraction from noisy backgrounds, as typified by many of the currently popular masking paradigms. The methods used most frequently require the subject to "detect" the stimulus; however, the meaning of "detection" in this stage is quite different from its use in the context of the luminosity thresholds of Stage 1. At this third stage of processing, all the component parts of the stimulus and the interfering visual noise are considerably above the absolute luminosity thresholds, as well as beyond (or excluded from) the constraining influences of the lateral interaction processes characteristic of Stage 2 processes. The subject's task in the latter case is to extract the components of the signal from those of the noise on the basis of some geometrical property of the signal that the noise does not possess. This may be done in spite of the fact that all components of both stimulus and noise are of the same luminosity, color, or even shape. Some property of geometrical organization is, therefore, critical at this stage to the discrimination of the signal from the background. Dot patterns have also been used to study this level of visual processing (Green, 1957; Uttal, 1969, 1970) and, indeed, it is at this level that the present study is directed.

In both Stages 2 and 3, visual processes are characterized by a strong dependence on the specific geometry of the stimulus. As such, they must be considered to be produced by neurological representations and interactions that are isomorphic to the original stimulus patterns. Stimulus dimensions, which were originally specified in terms of distances or other spatial relationships, must still be represented in a closely related manner at the neurological levels at which these stages of processing occur. It seems certain that topological constancy, at least, is required. Stages 1, 2, and 3 are therefore mediated by mechanisms that are still geometrically consistent with the original stimulus and may be said to be spatially "unencoded."

"Encoding," of course, has two meanings in contemporary psychobiology. The first deals with the neural representation of physical stimulus patterns by other patterns of electrochemical action in neurons. This change of energy state is assumed to initially take place immediately on transduction at the receptor and also at each successive neural level (see Uttal, 1973a, for a discussion of encoding of this sort). This type of neural encoding may or may not be dimensionally isomorphic. However, neural encoding is not presently considered here; instead, the topic is another form of encoding that has to do with the symbolic representation of visual information in perceiving organisms, one that involves dimensional changes that go far beyond topological isomorphism. Patterns in this context are encoded in ways that allow substantial changes or even total loss of the spatial dimensionality of the stimulus pattern. Once encoded in this manner, signals are dealt with in terms of their meaning or other symbolic significance rather than in terms of their original geometrical relations.

Stage 4. Processing of geometrical stimuli at Stage 4, the first level of symbolic representation, is undoubtedly accomplished by neural mechanisms that no longer represent the stimulus isomorphically. Instead, the stimulus is merely used as a system of cues to convey certain multidimensional information, and any one of several informationally equivalent, but not necessarily isomorphic, stimuli can do the same. The methodological emphasis employed to explore Stage 4 is also characteristically different. Masking is no longer used as the research tool; the emphasis is on the cognitive information-processing load created by the multiple dimensions of the stimulus pattern.

Therefore, although experiments that assay effects at Stage 4 may also use dot patterns very much like those used to assay phenomena of the preceding three stages (Garner, 1962; Garner & Clement, 1963), the specific geometrical details of the stimuli—so important in specifying Stage 3 phenomena—are no longer of consequence. Dot spacing, for example, has been found to be critical in studies of Stage 3 processes (Uttal, Bunnell, & Corwin, 1970) but apparently has little effect when attention is directed to Stage 4 processes (Garner, 1972, personal communication). Furthermore, at Stage 4, the geometry of the stimuli per se is no longer of any real significance and quite different patterns can convey the same information to the observer for cognitive processing of one sort or another. For example, Garner notes that dimensional effects studied with dot patterns of varied redundancy in the X and Y dimensions can just as easily be explored with plastic chips that vary redundancy by manipulating the dimensions of color and shape.

Stage 4 processes are, therefore, those that are concerned with the physical characteristics and spatial geometry of the stimulus only to the extent that these dimensions convey dimensional information. The limits of the stimulus to convey this information depend only on its ability to exceed the boundary conditions imposed by the first three stages of processing. The stimulus pattern must be detectable with regard to energy, uninhibited by its neighbors, and not hidden in any obscuring visual mask before Stage 4 processing can be studied in isolation from the effects of the earlier stages.

Stages 5 and 6. A fifth stage of visual processing may also be distinguished from the preceding ones. This stage, subsequent to the dimensional analysis described in Stage 4, concerns the classification of the detected, dimensionally processed information into stereotypical classes. Thus, once the relevant dimensions have been decoded, order can be introduced by the specification of categories on clusters with a common meaning. Finally, either the implicit act of perception or the explicit response itself may be considered as a possible sixth stage of processing. Clearly, the neural mechanisms involved in categorization of this perceptual response—the fourth, fifth, and sixth stages of visual processing—are far more complex than those underlying the geometrically isomorphic visual representation of the first three unencoded stages of processing.

In the present study, attention is specifically directed at Stage 3 types of processing. The problem of interest is the detection of ordered arrays of dots in fields of identical but randomly placed visual noise dots. The experimental method is a fairly familiar, typical masking paradigm in which the subject's task is to discriminate known and ordered arrays of dots from random masking patterns. All the dots are well above luminosity and acuity thresholds and, as noted, it seems relatively well established (see the discussion on the advantages of dots in Chapter 2, Section I.E) that at the dot spacings used there is no significant lateral interaction between the dots. No diminution in the apparent brightness of any dot has ever been observed to result from this combined signal and noise stimulus; all stimulus and noise dots are equally bright at equivalent portions of their time course.

Subsequent portions of this book review earlier theories of form detection, consider some new data and their implications, and then test a theoretical hypothesis originally suggested by Dodwell (1971) that offers considerable promise as a conceptual model of this kind of visual form detection. The last sections present a speculative, but plausible, neurophysiological model and an attempt to interpret the significance of the findings and the theory.

III. REVIEW OF EARLIER THEORIES OF FORM DETECTION

Any taxonomic review of form detection theories is complicated by a number of difficulties. At the outset, as noted above, several different stages or processes of perception have been somewhat uncritically mixed within a general rubric of recognition performance. In consequence, different theories of form perception often implicitly describe several different stages of the total form recognition problem simultaneously, even if this fact is not explicitly recognized by their authors. In addition, some models are solely descriptive or are concerned only with mathematical descriptions of the behavioral transforms relating stimulus pattern and response and so are patently nonphysiological. Furthermore, any attempt to categorize theories is difficult in that each theory may serve some role in several of the different categories of any taxonomy. For example, Gestalt theory is

III. EARLIER THEORIES OF FORM DETECTION

notably concerned with the global organizational or group properties of the stimulus, but some workers also have made specific assumptions about how these properties might be processed by what were once thought to be plausible neurophysiological mechanisms.

Moreover, many of the theories presented as distinct alternatives may turn out ultimately to be, in fact, quite similar. Some are similar in terms of the mathematical formalities. For example, power spectrum densities are formally related to autocorrelations by a single transform: each is the Fourier transform of the other. Others are interrelated because in some way they imply equivalent neural implementations or because they simply reflect different aspects of a single mechanism.

The classic example of apparently contradictory positions, of course, is the wave and quantum controversy that raged among the early twentieth century atomic physicists. What could have been more distinct from the notion that light is a particle than the idea that light is a wave? Yet no two theories have ever so effectively merged into each other to the benefit of each as the modern description of light as either a particle of a wave or a wave of particles. It is certainly the case, however, that the natural development of the theory of electromagnetic energy required the explicit formalization of each approach so that the exact meaning of both could be understood. Further understanding of significant importance was achieved when attempts were made to rationalize the photoelectric data and the diffraction data obtained from the experimental paradigms that were separately invoked in support of each theoretical position. In the same way, the various views of pattern recognition presented here are necessary and useful steps toward what ultimately must be the emergence of a single comprehensive description of how people see patterns.

It is necessary, however, to further delimit the scope of the discussion. The specific theories to be discussed are intentionally limited to those possessing structural assumptions in terms of either neural nets, mathematical formulations or analogies, or motor and performance variables. In general, the merely cognitive descriptions are not considered. In particular, attention is concentrated on those theories that are more relevant to the present concern with the Stage 3 type of detection process.

This also means, of course, that no attention is given to the considerable body of theorizing that occurred before the twentieth century. The interested reader may wish to look into Pastore's (1971) book for a comprehensive discussion and historical survey, or to Allport (1955) for an in-depth review of some of the more cognitive approaches. More contemporary reviews of form recognition theory have also been presented by Neisser (1967), Dodwell (1970), and Zusne (1970). Several important collections including a variety of theoretical positions have also been published in recent years. The reader's attention is specifically directed to those of Wathen-Dunn (1967), Uhr (1966), Watanabe (1969), Dodwell (1971), and Grüsser and Klinke (1971).

A. Sensory–Motor Theories

One recurrent theme linking form recognition theories is the suggestion that some aspect of a motor response elicited by the stimulus is necessary for the production of the perceptual experience. In many cases, the specific motor response invoked is the voluntary eye movement. Sensory–motor theories of this sort often appear to be based on two highly controversial assumptions. First, all sensory–motor theories implicitly assume that the percept can occur only if the component parts of a stimulus are scanned in a serial fashion. The necessity for the invocation of eye movements is either implicitly or explicitly based on the assumption that a complex pattern of multiple parts cannot be dealt with in a holistic way; that is, that parallel processing is not possible. Second, such theories also assume that the act of perception requires the occurrence of some motor response. Therefore, perception is considered to be not a direct result of the stimulus but rather an indirect concomitant of the motor processing of stimuli. Sensory motor theories of thought often make similar assumptions: we "think" to the extent that we subvocalize our mental processes with actual, although minute, laryngeal muscular contractions.

One of the most important and influential of the form recognition theories to invoke eye movements was that proposed by Hebb (1949). Hebb utilized eye movements as a vehicle for the establishment of the "phase sequence"—a temporal pattern of elicitation of cell assemblies, neurophysiological subsystems that themselves were thought to be the specific feature-sensitive units. Hebb dealt specifically with the triangle as an exemplar of his theory of perceptual development. He concentrated on corners as the criterion features for form recognition, which he apparently assumed were more or less innately tuned to specific cell assemblies. Hence, the eye movements were necessary to allow sequential fixations so that the corners could be fused into the single, learned percept "triangle." This fusing was presumed by Hebb to be mediated by the residual aftereffects of the successive fixations on the component corners.

Platt (1958, 1962) also invoked eye movements as a necessary mechanism. He based his theory on a different notion, namely, a "self-congruence" maintained by certain forms under various conditions of translation and rotation caused by displacements of the eye's line of view. The specific conditions of eye movement under which self-congruence is maintained is the key criterion for the perception of a particular geometrical form according to Platt.

Both these sensory–motor theories, and others that invoke eye movements as a necessary part of human form recognition, fall victim to a very simple counterargument: visual forms are detected and classified quite well in tachistoscopic exposures. Some sensory–motor theorists may fall back on "attentive scanning" of afterimages, but this position is also difficult to defend. In fact, almost nothing has been said that satisfactorily counters the tachistoscopic exposure argument against the eye movement hypothesis.

B. Neurophysiological Theories

A large group of theoretical formulations about the nature of form recognition has been based specifically on neurophysiological findings. These neurophysiologically based theories can be classified into three separate groups. First, some theoreticians, primarily those associated with the Gestalt school of psychology, have concentrated on the role of continuous fields of electrical activity (or their analogs) within the tissue of the brain. A second group has been concerned primarily with the specific sensitivities and feature-filtering properties of single cells. Still a third group has concentrated mainly on the effects of relatively unspecialized cells organized in logical networks that collectively possess specific processing capabilities.

1. Neurophysiological field theories.

Gestalt psychology accumulated a large amount of anecdotal and a modest amount of quantitative evidence to demonstrate that there were perceptual interactions between the different parts of a multicomponent visual stimulus. Some of the interactions appeared to be analogous but, of course, no suggestion was made that they were homologous to the action of magnetic or electrical fields of force. Because of the process analogies, there was a considerable impetus to the development of theories of pattern vision and interaction exhibiting the same sorts of continuous field effects found in those physical domains. Köhler (1929) was one of the most vigorous proponents of this notion and suggested specifically that the fields of interaction were mediated by the electronic spread of slowly varying, graded, electrochemical fields produced by the cumulative action of the mass of neurons in any chunk of brain tissue. Such theories were discarded when subsequent experiments showed that form perception in animals was maintained at high levels of performance despite drastic disruptions of the cortical electrical field structure produced by slicing the brain, inserting tantalum pins (Sperry, Miner, & Myers, 1955), or applying gold strips or pins (Lashley, Chow, & Semmes, 1951).

Although these studies seem quite definitive in their rejection of field interactions based on electrotonic spread, it must not be assumed that they also provide a basis for rejecting all neural field theories. The arrangement of neurons in the cerebrum of vertebrates is clearly one based on interactions among large numbers of discrete neurons. As larger and larger numbers of these discrete, yet highly interconnected, units are involved in any process, or as one's perspective enlarges to encompass increasingly molar behavior, the macroscopic concatenation of microscopic parts converges on a state that becomes increasingly difficult to differentiate from a continuous field. The work of such electrophysiologists as Fox and O'Brien (1965) clearly makes this point. They have shown how the statistics of single-cell responsiveness approaches the form of compound evoked potentials as the sample size grows.

III. EARLIER THEORIES OF FORM DETECTION

Other forms of field theory were also suggested. Some were most amusing analogies. Expressing many of the same reservations about current research directions as the two authors quoted at the beginning of this book, Blum (1967) described a transform he called the "medial axis function" (MAF), which he believed enhanced the global form aspects of a stimulus at the expense of local detail. The MAF transform, he proposed, was similar to the interactions that might occur among expanding waves of activity produced in a field by shaped wave generators. The main idea behind the MAF was that the transformation of the original complete spatial pattern into a small set of vectorlike components would allow a quantified comparison of a large set of geometrical forms.

Bittermann, Krauskopf, and Hochberg (1954) also have proposed a field type of theory that seeks to explain form thresholds by invoking processes analogous to the diffusion or growth patterns of bacterial colonies. They showed that growth patterns (i.e., the fields of growth) agreed to a certain degree with the detection thresholds for luminous forms of various shapes.

2. Single-cell neurophysiological theories. By far the most popular neurophysiological theories of form perception in recent years have been those based on the specific feature sensitivities of single cells at various levels of the vertebrate visual nervous system. This trend was initiated by the neurophysiological findings of lateral inhibition in the horseshoe crab eye (for example, Hartline, Wagner, & Ratliff, 1956; Hartline & Ratliff, 1957, 1958) and vigorously stimulated by the further discovery of feature-sensitive cells in the frog by Lettvin and his co-workers (Lettvin, Maturana, McCulloch, & Pitts, 1959) and by the work of Hubel and Wiesel on the cat and monkey (see, for example, Hubel & Wiesel, 1963, 1968). The magnitude and scope of subsequent work in this neurophysiological arena is impossible to sum up in a few words; the reader is directed to an especially succinct summary of what are called "trigger features" for a wide variety of neurons in several different animals (Barlow, Narasimhan, & Rosenfeld, 1972). The reader should particularly note their Figure 1 and Table 1, adaptations of which are reproduced in Table 1-1 here. The net impact of these important neurophysiological findings was to suggest to some psychologists that some processes

TABLE 1-1
Anatomical Locations and Specific Triggers of Feature-Sensitive Neurons in the Nervous Systems of Various Species[a]

Anatomical location	Trigger feature	Anatomical location	Trigger feature
Goldfish		*Cat* (main types)	
Retina	Local redness or greenness	Retina	Local brightening and dimming
	Directed movement		
Frog		Lateral geniculate	Local brightening and dimming
Retina	Convex edge	Visual cortex Area 17	
	Sustained edge	Simple cells	Moving, slits, bars, edges with specific orientation
	Changing contrast		
	Dimming	Complex cells	Combinations of simple cell outputs of same orientation
	Dark		
Optic tectum	Newness	Visual cortex Area 18	
	Sameness	Hypercomplex I cells	Ends of lines
	Binocularity	Hypercomplex II cells	Line segments and corners
Pigeon			
Retina	Directed movement		
	Oriented edges		

Ground squirrel

Retina	Local brightening or dimming
	Local blueness or greenness
	Directed movement
Lateral geniculate body	Color-coded units
Optic tectum	Directional units
	Oriented slits or bars
	Complex units

Rabbit

Retina	Local brightening or dimming
	Directed movement
	Fast or slow movement
	Edge detectors
	Oriented slits or bars
	Uniformity detectors
Lateral geniculate	Greater directional selectivity
Tectum	Habituating units

Cat (infrequent types)

Retina	Directed movement
	Uniformity detectors
Lateral geniculate	Local blueness or greenness
	Binocular, directional, and orientational units
Optic tectum	Directed movement
	Complex units

Monkey

Retina	Local brightening or dimming
Lateral geniculate	Local redness, greenness, or blueness
	Various forms of color coding
Cortex	Similar to cat; some color coded
Inferotemporal cortex	Very complex; possible hand detector

[a] Adapted from Barlow et al. (1972); copyright American Association for the Advancement of Sciences.

which had been handled only descriptively, at best, by earlier form recognition theories might be explained by hypothesizing analogous properties of single neurons in the human visual system.

Some of the earliest examples of the application of these ideas were relatively straightforward. McCullough (1965) reported what she believed to be a perceptual analog to the sensitivity of the Hubel and Wiesel directionally preferential cells when she described color adaptation effects of hypothesized edge detectors. Andrews (1965), basing his conclusions mostly on preferred perceived orientations in a psychophysical experiment, also pointed out a number of functional similarities between his data and the Hubel and Wiesel results. Blakemore and Sutton (1969) reflected an analogous, though reverse, direction in their theorizing when they noted that grating adaptation experiments might allow a means for "the study of the trigger features of optimum stimuli of human sensory neurons."

Mayzner's group (Buchsbaum & Mayzner, 1969; Mayzner & Tresselt, 1970; Mayzner, Tresselt, & Helfer, 1967) has vigorously supported the notion that lateral inhibitory interaction between cortical columns of neurons is responsible for the "sequential blanking" effects found in their experiments. They hypothesize a form of interaction between columns that is not only specific to the direction of line movement (as reported by Hubel and Wiesel) but that must be interpreted as sensitivity to the number of sides in a stimulus polygon or even as sensitivity to word meaning.

Campbell and Kulikowski (1966), examining the effect of orientation on visual resolution, also linked their data to the Hubel and Wiesel type of preferred directional sensitivities. Noting that "it is, of course, not possible to argue convincingly from psychophysical data to neurophysiological descriptions of the visual system," they found that some characteristics of the Hubel and Wiesel data were very similar to some of the data obtained in their experiment, not only qualitatively but also in the details of the range of angles of sensitivity of the compared effects.

Dember and Purcell (1967) argued that the Hartline type of lateral inhibition was the most likely candidate to explain certain perceptual disinhibition effects they have observed. However, the most formal theoretical position in this area was taken by Weisstein (1968). She has developed a very compelling mathematical model for masking

III. EARLIER THEORIES OF FORM DETECTION

effects, based on notions of lateral inhibitory interaction between neurons at both the central and peripheral levels. Rothberg (1968) has also used Weisstein's (1966, 1968) data to develop a computer model based on similar notions of lateral inhibitory interaction.

In spite of all this attention, however, it should be noted that no really substantial linkage has yet been established between molar visual behavior and findings at the unicellular neurophysical level. Indeed, when specific comparisons are made, it often turns out that the initial analogy does not stand up. (See particularly Uttal, 1971, and Weisstein, 1969, for a discussion of this important conceptual issue.)

Although the emphasis in the application of this neurophysiological data to psychological theory has been on the function of single cells, there is one aspect of the work that does bridge the gap to the next stage in our discussion. Hubel and Wiesel have defined a hierarchy of cells of increasing complexity and suggest, in some instances (for example, Hubel & Wiesel, 1962), the nature of the interconnections that may exist between simple cells, for example, and cells of the next higher order of complexity. They thus explain how the response characteristics of the latter may be built on those of the former. This hierarchy of cell types may be related to the stages of visual processing described above.

3. Neural network theories. In contrast to the preceding class of neurophysiological form recognition theories, which stress highly specialized unicellular trigger features, there is another class that emphasizes quite a different fundamental assumption. That assumption is based on the interaction within networks of relatively unspecialized neurons. The authors of these theories treat their neural elements very much as general-purpose building blocks, just as is done in logical design by electronic circuit engineers, and the special information-processing properties of the network are attributed to the manner in which these blocks are interconnected rather than to the properties of the units. The innovator of this theme in form recognition theory was probably the landmark paper by Pitts and McCulloch (1947). More modern developments (Deutsch, 1955; Dodwell, 1957, as summarized by Dodwell, 1970; Sutherland, 1957) have brought this line of theory to a relatively high level of development.

Barlow and Levick's (1965) discussion of their neurophysiological findings concerning direction sensitivity in the rabbit retina is also certainly a member of this same class.

Whereas it is clear that this network approach must be congruent with at least certain aspects of the internal mechanism of the nervous system, there is a major epistemological difficulty faced by these investigators that has not yet been handled satisfactorily. This difficulty is the general problem of the multiple solutions that are possible when one tries to mechanically interpret the internal workings of a "black box." If information is limited solely to input and output considerations, no proof of the uniqueness of any given solution to the problem of internal construction is possible. Many different networks, built from a variety of component subsets, are eligible candidates for the mechanization of even the simplest sort of response. Considering the relative simplicity of the pattern recognition tasks now being explained on the basis of network interaction by these theories, it does not seem difficult to generate a number of alternative but equally plausible networks. Indeed, two alternative networks are considered in Barlow and Levick's (1965) paper: one network based on a summatory interaction and one on an inhibitory interaction. Each is able to simulate the directional sensitivity of the rabbit retina but on the basis of quite opposite principles of interaction.

However obvious this fact of nonunique solutions may be, in this case, where the nature of the "black box" is quite explicit, the reader should appreciate that this is also a fundamental problem with all other models that speculate about the structure of some underlying mechanism for which only input–output information is available. Specifically, this includes the model to be presented in this study and all of the other related theories described in this section.

C. Computational Network Theories

The neural network theories usually make another specific assumption about the elements of the network. As a group, neural network theories strive to maximize the ways in which their constituent elements mimic true neuronal properties. Another group of theories has grown up in a somewhat different context—the artificial intelligence field—which does not strive for the same sort of biological mimicry. Instead, the latter theories are characterized more by an emphasis

III. EARLIER THEORIES OF FORM DETECTION

on the network arrangement than by the pseudoneuronal properties of the elements. This class of theory is considered under the rubric of "computational network theories" because models of this sort usually have been embodied in computer programs. In fact, however, they are often nonnumerical, if not noncomputational. The digital computer or analog circuit used to simulate these models is more often used as a logical or simulation tool than as a numerical manipulator.

One of the notions to gain considerable currency in this field is that of the random net. In the neural network theories described above, highly specific patterns of interconnection are typically assumed to be necessary for the circuits to do their job and the units are assumed to be interconnected on the basis of some prior ontogenetic development or experiential plasticity. In view of some computational network theorists, however, such regular organization is not necessary. Stemming mainly from studies in perceptual development or adaptive automata, a number of form recognition theories have been developed that assume only random connections among the neural units of their networks.

Rosenblatt (1958) was one of the first to suggest a randomly connected, neuronlike model of form recognition. His system, known as a "perceptron," consists of three layers of neural elements. The first layer is composed of a mosaic of receptor units. These receptor units are connected to a layer of association units, which in turn are connected to a layer of response units. The system is designed to allow adaptive adjustment of weighting valences between the input receptor units and the output response units by training processes analogous to human learning. The sensitivities of the connections between the three layers are modified by experience in such a way that a particular input pattern becomes associated with a particular output pattern. (A full discussion of perceptronlike mechanisms can be found in Minsky & Papert, 1969).

Other forms of computational network theories not involving random interconnections have also been proposed. Selfridge's (1959) "pandemonium" model of a form recognizer, for example, although not a random net, does share many common features with Rosenblatt's perceptron. Its operation also depends on the evaluation of outputs of a large number of feature detectors by means of a set of analyzers or decision units. This same type of organization is also shared by Uhr and Vossler's (1963) model, although a different sort of feature recognizer is used in Uhr's theory than in Selfridge's.

Another sort of computational form recognition process is exemplified by the work of Rosenfeld, Thomas, and Lee (1969) and of Montanari (1971). None is concerned with modeling specific neural nets; each proposes a picture-processing algorithm that extracts patterns from a noisy environment. Each could be mechanically implemented in the same way as the neural nets mentioned above. Rosenfeld and his colleagues have suggested a local processing algorithm capable of extracting dotted patterns from dotted background noise on the basis of local dot densities. Clearly, because this local processing algorithm is in many ways incongruent with human capabilities, it cannot truly represent the human form recognition process. One of the most serious weaknesses, of course, is that the detector is sensitive only to local densities and is totally insensitive to the global form of the pattern. Consequently, the algorithm suggested by Rosenfeld and his colleagues detects a curved line equally as well as a dotted line and shows no special sensitivity to any particular form. It has been known since the Gestalt days that this feature of their line detector is not characteristic of human form recognition. The concatenation of this model with modern neurophysiological and psychophysical data in the paper by Barlow *et al.* (1972) is therefore somewhat misleading in that the computer technique, the neurophysiological data, and the physiological data do not agree even to a first approximation, despite the fact that all deal with some aspect of form detection.

Montanari's (1971) algorithm, in contrast, does take into account nonlocal properties of patterns in noise and so can be expected to be sensitive to some sorts of global geometry, similar to the way that people respond. Indeed, another advantage of Montanari's work is that the global algorithms allow relatively large gaps to be bridged. This is a feature well beyond the capability of local processing algorithms.

Although these are the computational network form recognition theories best known among psychologists, a large number of similar processes have been utilized by computer scientists to process pictorial information. Even a brief survey of these varied algorithms is impossible here, but the reader is directed to Brick (1969) for a consideration of the many kinds of image transformation and decision algorithms that have been invented in that field. Watanabe (1969) and Meisel (1972) are important sources for information concerning the more mathematical considerations in the field of computational form recognition.

Although many of these computational algorithms are ingenious, the impression one immediately develops is that they neither provide an adequate model of human behavior nor adequately do the job for which they have been designed. It appears that no form of mathematical analysis is yet completely suitable for simulating stimulus arrangement or organization in the manner in which humans process such information.

D. Correlation Theories

Finally, there is a group of theories using a correlational type of mathematical formularization that has enjoyed great popularity during the last decade. All these models are tied together by a common mathematical formula, and it is often said that they are formally identical to each other. With regard to the specific theories, that statement is an exaggeration, for each of the different approaches uniquely emphasizes one or another specific implementation or mechanism of the correlational process. For example, if one were to separately implement both an autocorrelator and a cross-correlator, the two devices would be structurally different despite the fact that a common mathematical vehicle can be used to describe both.

However, certain specific links do exist between one or another of these formularizations that make them functionally if not mechanistically equivalent. For example, it is well established that the autocorrelation function and the power density spectrum are Fourier transforms of each other; the output of each transform contains the same parts of the original information as the other. It is entirely possible that other similar equivalences, not yet explicitly identified, exist between alternate models of the pattern recognition process. What each of the theories discussed below does individually is to suggest an alternative neural implementation specific to each mathematical formulation.

The general correlational formula for two-dimensional spaces, as exemplified in the present case by the visual field, can be represented as

$$\phi(x, y) = \iint f(x, y) \cdot g(x, y) \, dx \, dy, \qquad (1\text{-}1)$$

where $\phi(x, y)$ is defined as the general correlational transform of the function $f(x, y)$ with another function $g(x, y)$. If $f(x, y)$ is the stimulus pattern, then the specific nature of $g(x, y)$ selects the particular type of correlational process from among the family of related transforms described by the general equation.

1. Cross correlation. If $g(x, y)$ is simply another pattern unrelated to $f(x, y)$, then the $\phi(x, y)$ is the cross-product correlation (although in two dimensions rather than one) so familiar in statistical analysis. When two geometric forms are correlated in this manner, the process is, in fact, embodying what is less generally known as a "template-matching model" of form recognition. The key notion in any template match is that a number of these correlations are computed between $f(x, y)$ and a set of $g(x, y)$ templates. The particular $g(x, y)$ that produces the highest $\phi(x, y)$ is considered to be the best matching prototype. Therefore, the classification and categorization aspects of form recognition are immediately obtained by simply identifying the highest $\phi(x, y)$ and determining which template has given that maximum $\phi(x, y)$.

One particularly well-explicated theory of form recognition, based on a cross-correlation between input test patterns and a set of stored templates, is described by Kabrisky (1966). His stored templates are themselves transforms of the original prototypes, but the basic principle is the same—a comparison between the test stimulus and a set of reference templates. Simmons (1971) has also suggested that a cross-correlation process is the basis of the bat's echo-ranging capability. Julesz (1971) invokes cross-correlation mechanisms to explain depth perception and Bell and Lappin (1973) propose that similar neural processors underlie human discrimination of motion.

2. Fourier analysis. If $g(x, y)$ represents any of a set of sinusoidal functions in space, however, then $\phi(x, y)$ becomes equivalent to a spatial Fourier analysis of the original stimulus pattern. Pollen,

III. EARLIER THEORIES OF FORM DETECTION

Lee, and Taylor (1971) have explicitly expressed this sort of thinking in their application of Fourier analysis to explain the considerable body of both electrophysiological data (for example, Campbell, Cooper, & Enroth-Cugel, 1969; Campbell, Cooper, Robson, & Sachs, 1969; Campbell & Maffei, 1970; Enroth-Cugel & Robson, 1966) and psychophysical data (for example, Blakemore, Nachmias, & Sutton, 1970; Campbell, Nachmias, & Jukes, 1970; Campbell & Robson, 1968; Gilinsky, 1968; Sachs, Nachmias, & Robson, 1971; Weisstein & Bisaha, 1972) that seem to indicate that some sort of spatial frequency analysis is being carried out in the mammalian visual process. Walsh transforms, which use a set of square-wave, orthogonal functions instead of the sine waves used in Fourier analysis, have also been used as predictors of human pattern perception by Goble (1975).

It should be noted that much of the current discussion of laser models of optical image processing is also framed in these same mathematical terms. The use of optical Fourier analysis and image processing to filter our particular properties using the interaction of wavefronts of coherent light clearly represents only one alternative means of carrying out the computations represented by Eq. (1-1). Diffraction patterns produced by passing coherent light through transparencies (Lendaris & Stanley, 1970) are also a closely allied transform. Indeed, diffraction patterns in general can be considered to be nothing more than spatial Fourier transforms of the original stimulus pattern.

Curiously, this same approach to form recognition also characterized the thoughts of a distinguished psychologist long before either spatial frequency models were used in this context or the laser was introduced as a computational tool. In 1942, Lashley suggested that interference patterns between waves of neural activity, akin to the interaction of optical diffraction patterns, might be set up in large portions of the brain. The extent and shape of these patterns, he believed, were related to the observer's perception of a form. This idea, of course, is an extension of the less specific ideas of Gestalt theorists and is closely related to the global field theories mentioned above. It is also closely related to some of the notions of autocorrelation that are discussed below and a similar concept can serve as an important conceptual bridge between many different form recognition theories.

3. Feature detection. If $g(x, y)$ is some special characteristic that is a subcomponent or "feature" of the original stimulus pattern, then the computation of $\phi(x, y)$ essentially serves as a feature-filtering process for the selective enhancement of that particular feature of $f(x, y)$. Expressed in this way, it is clear that such an application of Eq. (1-1) would implement a sort of feature-filtering or feature-sensitive pattern-recognition process similar to that suggested by the single-cell models described above. However, in this case, feature filtering is not based on the specific sensitivities of a single neuron but on the evaluation of a specific mathematical algorithm by what could be, in principle, a homogeneous and isotropic sheet of neurons with regard to a possible neural implementation. Therefore, a basic and essential difference prevails between all correlational theories and any theory stressing cellular feature sensitivity.

4. Averaging. If $g(x, y)$ is merely a periodic impulse, however, the correlation process is closely related to simple statistical averaging—a sequential process that extracts periodic or repetitive aspects of a periodic stimulus at the expense of the aperiodic components or noise.

5. Other transforms. Many other mathematical functions have been used as $g(x)$. Prewitt (1970) has reviewed a number of the more esoteric forms in a most informative tutorial chapter on optical image processing. She notes that image restoration, enhancement, and extraction are frequently required in various information-processing fields today; and the mathematical models that represent these processes also can be considered as indirect models of human form recognition. Such functions as Chebyshev polynomials and Bessel functions have been used by various workers in the general correlational equation. Each of these transforms has some special advantage that makes it particularly appropriate in certain applications.

6. Autocorrelation. Finally, if $g(x, y)$ is nothing more than a spatially shifted version of $f(x, y)$ of the form $f(x + n \Delta x, y + m \Delta y)$, where n and m are integers and Δx and Δy are unit "shifts," then Eq. (1-1) represents the the two-dimensional spatial autocorrelation

III. EARLIER THEORIES OF FORM DETECTION

of the stimulus pattern. Autocorrelation models of this sort have many characteristics that make them especially attractive descriptions of human pattern recognition, as is shown below.

Autocorrelation functions, it should be noted, have been applied previously in a number of instances to human form recognition. Perhaps the first published instance is Licklider's (1959) suggestion that some sort of neurological autocorrelator may be responsible for our ability to hear combination tones that themselves possess no physical energy—a clear contradiction of the generally accepted place theories of neural coding in audition. His model is essentially a one-dimensional autocorrelator operating on a quasi-periodic time series (the acoustic stimulus pattern). Licklider is specific in detailing the sort of neural circuitry that is required to implement such a system.

Cherry (1961) also invokes a similar sort of autocorrelating preprocessor as a preliminary to a cross-correlating binaural fusion model. Reichardt (1961) is another who has used autocorrelation mechanisms in a single dimension to model the optomotor responses of a beetle exposed to a time-varying sequence of light and dark stripes by means of a rotating drum.

More recently, Engel (1969) has also suggested that autocorrelation functions may exist in the retina and may be contributing factors in specifying the brightness of binocular luminance mixes when the two autocorrelated signals are cross-correlated. Engel, Dougherty, and Jones (1973) have extended some of these ideas to a study of character recognition in which noise-free alphabetic character stimuli were briefly exposed in a tachistoscope. They develop further a combined autocorrelational and cross-correlational explanation of recognitions and confusions between alphabetic characters. They assume that the retina autocorrelates the characters to transform them into a form in which the information (organizational) values are emphasized. Recognition scores, they have predicted, are correlated with the autocorrelational values, and confusion errors among the stimuli are associated with cross correlations between the autocorrelations for each figure.

Anderson (1968) also invoked autocorrelational principles when he described the first perceptual stages of a generalized model of memory. His comment, "Thus, the problem of recognition becomes the problem of detecting the presence of the autocorrelation of the input function in the spatial cross-correlation," is conceptually identical to the theme expressed in the present book. Anderson, in many of his later papers (1970, 1972, 1973), also speaks eloquently to the same general point to be made in Chapter 4, namely, that distributed, parallel processing networks are a plausible alternative to the single cell feature-filter hypothesis which has such wide currency in contemporary psychobiology.

Autocorrelation mechanisms in human vision were also proposed by Glass (1969), but on the basis of a demonstration that appears to reflect the properties of a transformed stimulus more than it does the properties of the perceiver. Glass also suggested that the autocorrelation is actually performed by single cell line detectors in the nervous system.

It should also be noted that autocorrelation has been proposed as a mechanism for computer pattern recognition and not specifically as a model of human pattern perception. Horwitz and Shelton (1961) used both digital and optical autocorrelators in their effort to automate character recognition processes for computer input.

Dodwell (1971) has also applied the autocorrelation function to visual problems very much like those considered in this study. In fact, he specifically suggests that the autocorrelation function may be an excellent description of the kind of dot-mixing experiments being reported here. Much of the discussion and explanation of the findings considered here have been stimulated by Dodwell's report, although there are a number of points in which differences of view become obvious (for example, differences concerning the relevance of contours, autocorrelation and eye movements, and the physiological basis of the transform). Nonetheless, the theoretical analysis in the present work is founded on his suggestions as well as on discussions with the author's colleagues James O. Chinnis, Jr., Joseph Mezrich, and Lawrence Goble.

In summary, the different theories discussed are presented either as specific models of the human pattern recognition process or as ones that mechanically simulate similar information-processing paradigms.

III. EARLIER THEORIES OF FORM DETECTION

It must be emphasized that many of the latter artificial pattern recognizers are not explicit models of the human pattern recognition process; nevertheless, they often provide insights to plausible ways in which this process may be implemented in the human.

An important question facing the reader is whether or not these various theories are really different from each other. So often in the history of science it has turned out that every theorist is at least partially correct, and that what appear originally to be mutually inconsistent theoretical approaches can be resolved by showing how each is, in fact, a view of a different aspect of a single problem. Similarities among the correlation-type theories have already been cited above, and although it is important to stress the fact again that even total formal identity is not tantamount to identity of implementation, there certainly is a common thread of integration and cross multiplication running through all of these processes. Indeed, the sensory–motor theories may also be gathered under this same umbrella, for in their stress on eye movement mechanisms each represents what can be legitimately interpreted as just another way in which one or another of the correlation theories can be implemented. Similarly, the neurophysiological theories, whether emphasizing fields or emphasing units, may be viewed as means of providing a biological implementation for correlation types of processes that also may eventually be formally described someday by such formulas as Eq. (1-1).

The correlation mathematics, however, can be at best only an approximation. Mathematical techniques have evolved to, and are still in, a state of development that is constrained by current application and contemporary means of evaluating algorithms. There is little justification for supposing that the correlation mathematics, which evolved in a completely different context to serve a completely different need, is the end solution to the discrete network interactions found in as complicated a mechanism as the human brain simply because of its convenience and availability. It should also be appreciated that the autocorrelation transform that is championed here is only one example of a process that operates on certain features of the stimulus, in a manner that reflects the properties of the stimulus features rather than those of the transformational mathematics. That is, the actual biological information-processing mechanism may not be a correlator per se but simply another process that is also responsive to the same features of the stimulus as the autocorrelator. What this model does is to emphasize that alternative approaches to the contemporary single-cell or spatial frequency feature-selective theories are viable. Specifically, to the degree that the autocorrelation model is successful, it supports the notion that a homogeneous sheet of unspecialized elements can also produce the specific feature sensitivities observed in neurophysiological and psychophysical experiments.

Another apparently controversial point that may prove to be only a superficial inconsistency concerns those theories which emphasize single cells as opposed to those which emphasize fields. The actual role of a single cell may be considerably different than the one in which it is usually cast. For example, the Hubel and Wiesel type of cells, simple or complex, may not represent the feature detectors themselves but may reflect one output of a feature-detecting mechanism composed of fieldlike networks of neurons. In other words, the activation of a given Hubel and Wiesel cell may be a response (just as the molar perception of an oriented grating is a response) to a particular set of stimulus conditions rather than a unicellular, feature-filtering analyzer.

If that is the case, and if single-cell sensitivities are ultimately shown to be only concomitant responses, then the nature of the neural ensemble may become of primary importance. It becomes clear on accepting this notion that the remaining controversy between highly specialized and relatively unspecialized neurons in the processing nets is of secondary importance. In sum, the theories reviewed here are probably not so much competitive as they are interactive and, perhaps, equivalent.

2
The Psychophysical Experiments

I. GENERAL METHOD OF PRESENT EXPERIMENTS

A. Subjects

The subjects participating in our experimental program were undergraduate students. Each experiment used at least four subjects who served for 1 hr a day, for which they were paid an hourly stipend. Typically, more than 400 responses were accumulated during each hour. As each subject served for 2 hr in each condition, about 3200 responses were pooled to estimate each plotted point in most of the figures to be presented. Over the 2-year experimental period, the same group of four subjects participated in each experiment, but many different groups (of four subjects each) participated in all 12 of the experiments. Large differences between separate groups of subjects were common and, therefore, absolute differences between experiments are probably not meaningful.

B. Apparatus

The general experimental procedure has utilized a visual masking paradigm in which target or signal forms, made up of organized patterns of dots, have been masked by varying numbers of randomly placed noise dots. Figure 2-1 exemplifies one of the stimulus patterns embedded in three densities of random visual noise depicting the progressive decline in detectability that occurs as the number of masking dots increases.

The dotted stimuli and visual noise were generated by the same small laboratory digital control computer that also carried out many of the decision-making, input, and output tasks necessary for complete execution of the experiment. Digitally encoded information, representing two-dimension positional coordinates (x and y) for each dot, were converted to analog voltage levels appropriate for the inputs of an ordinary laboratory oscilloscope (Tektronix Type 601). A Z axis signal, consisting of an 8-μsec pulse, was emitted by the computer to intensify a spot on the face of the phosphor after a delay of 6 μsec that enabled the signal inputs to the oscilloscope to stabilize. The phosphor on the CRT was a Type P-15, specially selected for its very brief persistence. The trace of an intensified spot diminished (according to the manufacturer's specifications) to 0.1% of its original brightness in less than 50 μsec. Therefore, each dot, whether noise or signal, lasted for this brief period of time, although the total duration of an entire stimulus burst could last as long as 3 msec. This maximum duration was produced by the minimum amount of computer processing time required to seek, store, and display the total number of dots (signal plus noise) present in any given stimulus.

The computer served many different roles in the experiment. It calculated anew and stored the random positions of the noise dots for presentation in each trial; it stored the nonrandom stimulus patterns in appropriate tables and randomly selected the specific one to be presented on each trial; it carried out all timing and clocking functions between the various portions of a single trial, as well as

I. GENERAL METHOD OF PRESENT EXPERIMENTS

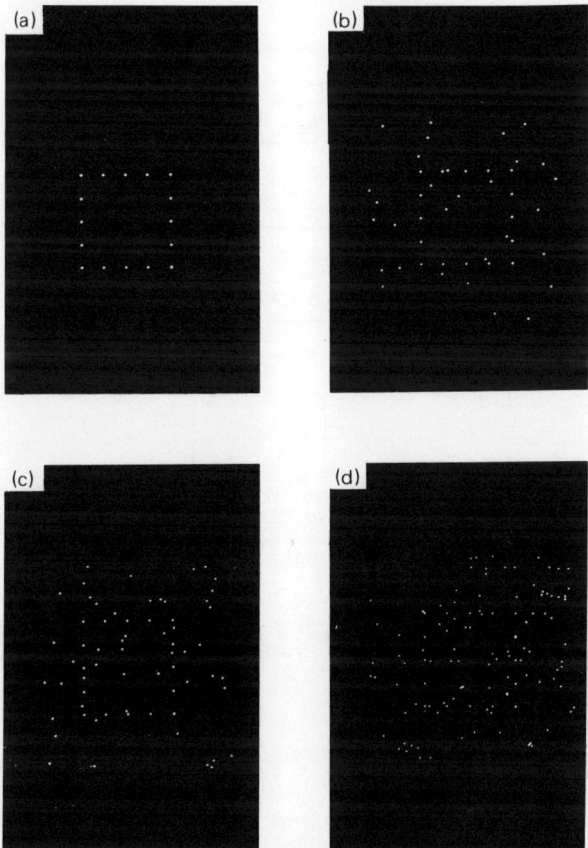

FIGURE 2-1 A dotted square presented in four different levels of random dotted noise. Stimulus displays have the appearance of one of these to the subject in the experiments reported in this study: (a) no masking dots, (b) 30 masking dots, (c) 50 masking dots, and (d) 100 masking dots. Note the progressive decline in the detectability of the target square as the number of masking dots increases.

between trials. It also acquired responses from the subject and provided a preliminary statistical evaluation at the end of each hourly session, along with a statistical summary of all runs at the end of each day.

The subject was seated in an acoustically shielded and darkened booth with his head movement constrained by a forehead rest at a

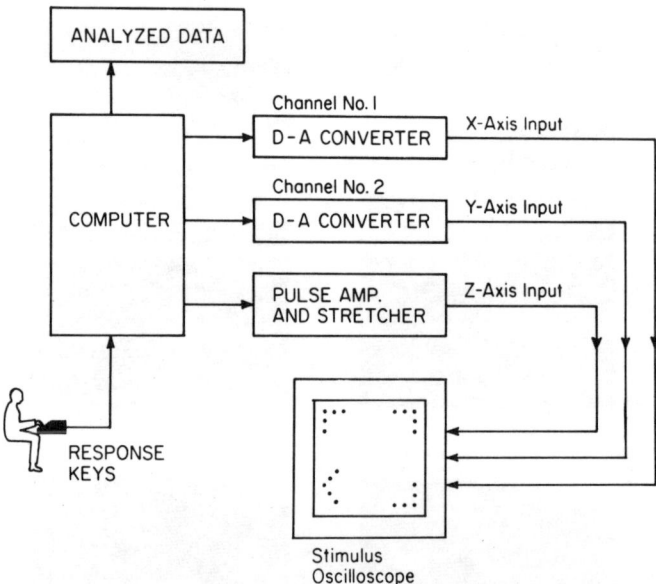

FIGURE 2-2 Block diagram of the equipment used in the present study. The computer generates stimuli by converting digital coordinates to analog voltages and analyzes responses acquired from a set of response keys.

distance of 13 inches from the face of the oscilloscope. In most experiments, a 1.5 × 1.5 inch area was masked on the face of the oscilloscope, defining a visual angle of 6.5° × 6.5°. Random noise dots might occur in any position within this square field, but the target forms, which varied from experiment to experiment, were slightly smaller—typically about 3° × 3°. The noise dots immediately followed the presentation of the target forms in all except the last experiment in this study. In that case, it either preceded or followed the target form, but always in separate hourly sessions. The arrangement of the experimental equipment is shown in Figure 2-2.

C. Procedure

The psychophysical procedure used in most of the experiments (note exceptions in Figures 2-3, 2-17, and 2-33) was a two-alternative, forced-choice design in which the subject was required to specify which of two sequential bursts, separated by 1.0 sec, contained both the target form and random visual noise, as opposed to the burst containing only random noise dots. The computer also randomly determined whether the target form would appear in the first or in the second noise burst; it then corrected the number of dots in the random noise of the nontarget burst by adding to it the number of random dots equal to the number of dots in the target form. This precaution eliminated the possibility that the subject might have been basing his decision on some extraneous variable, such as the overall brightness of the display or the overall dot numerosity, rather than on the intended variable of geometric form.

After two stimulus bursts, the subject responded by depressing one of two hand-held pushbuttons to indicate his decision. This response was acquired by the computer and, after a half-second delay, a "+" or a "−" feedback signal was plotted for 0.5 sec on the face of the oscilloscope to indicate to the subject whether or not his previous response had been correct. After the feedback signal, a delay of 1.0 sec occurred before the next trial was initiated. The cycle then repeated itself. The feedback signal also served to stabilize the subject's fixation.

In the experiments reported here, the major independent variables were the density of the noise dots and the geometry of the stimulus. Noise dot density was specified daily when the computer program was loaded and the experiment was being set up. The geometry variable was introduced by designing, encoding, and then reading in at load time a specific table containing the desired stimulus set. Dot luminosity was adjusted to approximately 0.5 cd/m^2 each day. However, many related studies have shown that stimulus intensity plays only a minimal role in this dot-masking paradigm.

The dependent variable throughout the entire series of experiments was the percentage of the total number of forms presented that were correctly detected. Whenever a two-alternative, forced-choice procedure was used, 50% represented chance performance levels.

D. Unique Attributes of the Dot-Masking Technique

A common methodological feature linking these experiments is that the stimulus and masking materials are made up entirely of organized patterns of the simplest possible form of stimulus—pinpointlike bright dots on a dark background. Because briefly exposed small dots interact with each other so weakly (a conclusion well established by von Békésy, 1968), the detection and recognition of dotted stimulus forms in this kind of dotted noise is almost purely a function of signal-to-noise ratios, in a way that is quite different from the type of interactions observed when continuous contours are near each other or when bright flashes make dimmer ones.

Although it is all too easy to refer glibly to "signal-to-noise" ratios, it is not so easy to define exactly which dimension of the dotted pattern is being divided by which other dimension; the term is therefore used a bit cryptically here. Dot density or numerosity clearly is not the only factor involved. Indeed, the determination of the set of multiple dimensions that define a signal is one of the major goals of this study. Each experiment performed is a test of whether or not a given attribute of an organized dotted stimulus is itself a contributor to its detectability and to the observer's specification of its properties as a "signal."

Because of their unique advantages, dotted stimulus materials have been used in a number of different experimental situations in recent years. Julesz (as summarized in Julesz, 1971) and Ross and Hogben (1974) applied dotted stimuli to the study of three-dimensional vision mediated by pure stereopsis, Garner and Clement (1963) have applied them to the study of figural goodness, and Eriksen and Collins (1968) have used them in the study of the fusion of quasi-random patterns into meaningful images. The type of dot-masking method used in this study was used earlier by Green (1957, 1963) in studies of radar tracking performance and by French (1954) in studies of target detection. Similar masking procedures have been devised using blur (Fry, 1957), noisy random histograms (Fitts, Weinstein, Rappaport, Anderson, & Leonard, 1956), and other forms of noisy backgrounds (Weisz, 1957; Crook, 1957) to study related problems. Much of this earlier work is summarized in a monograph edited by Wulfeck and Taylor (1957). But, as the years go by, it appears increasingly certain that dot masking may assay perceptual mechanisms that are quite different than those measured by these other methods.

The main reason for the use of dotted stimuli, and the source of their unique contribution to perceptual research, is that the dot pattern simplifies an extremely complex situation. Results of earlier work (for example, Eriksen & Collins, 1968; Uttal, 1969) seem to be consistent with the notion that the confusion of the dots, of both the stimulus and noise patterns, is the dominant factor in the Stage 3 effects—the main concern of this study. As such, studies of Stage 3 processes come very close to being analogs of signal detection problems encountered more often in auditory research. From this point of view, our experiments using dot patterns may have only superficial similarity to visual processes studied with other forms of sequential visual stimulation, for instance, the metacontrast paradigm, to which they bear a paradigmatic resemblance. In the case of metacontrast and masking with bright flashes, apparent brightness shifts do occur. Similarly, there are substantial differences between dot-masking effects and masking that involves bright masking flashes. Still, dot masking may share some common mechanisms with the parts of Schiller's (1965) or Turvey's (1973) work in which random patterns of lines are used as a mask, and with Kinsbourne and Warrington's (1962) and Haber and Standing's (1969) work with other kinds of visual noise. Nevertheless, differences in results obtained suggest that these various kinds of masking may not in fact assay identical visual mechanisms.

Schiller (1968, 1969), Kahneman (1968), and Fitzgerald (1970) also stressed the existence of a wide variety of visual retroactive inhibitory interaction effects. Evidently, several of the effects mentioned above are often intermixed in masking experiments. All the more, then, the fact that dot patterns allow the experimenter to abstract, in an effective way, a relatively pure portion of this complex of processes makes this method advantageous.

E. Specific Advantages of the Dot-Masking Technique

What, then, are the specifiable advantages of the dotted masking paradigm? A list of the more salient advantages must certainly include the following.

1. Dot patterns allow the experimenter to emphasize the factors of organization and arrangement that define a form, as opposed to merely the visibility or significance of the individual component of the form. Hints that such is the proper emphasis of research have

been made repeatedly over the years by Gestalt psychologists and by specialists in reading and speech perception. Words are perceived as molar forms rather than comprehended from detailed examinations of the component characters or phonemes. Likewise, the dot is the minimal—the *reductio ad simplicitum*—component with the fewest intrinsic properties of its own to interfere with the study of the organizational effects that are of first importance in perceptual phenomena.

2. With dot patterns, there is no sequential stimulation of the same receptors. The relative sparseness of the dots, even when noise levels are quite high, makes it improbable that the same locus will be stimulated twice in the same trial. The key point in this statement is that the absence of sequential stimulation of the same receptors means that the effects measured belong not to the photochemical realm of Stage 1 processes, but to the realm of geometric and organizational effects of an intermediate Stage 3 of visual information processing. Because the geometry is still critical, obviously the symbolic processes of the later stages are also excluded.

3. Dotted patterns and dotted noise are both weak stimuli for eliciting responses from contour-sensitive systems (Held, 1970; Uttal, 1970). This means that Stage 2 contour-sensitive systems within the visual system are largely excluded from whatever is assayed by the dot-masking technique.

4. No lateral inhibitory interaction among dots is elicited by this procedure, for two reasons. First, small dots at suprathreshold luminosities spatially interact only very weakly. This result has been confirmed by many workers, specifically, von Békésy (1968), who noted:

> . . . it can be demonstrated that stimuli with a small spread do not produce large changes in the local sensation as a consequence of inhibition. If the stimuli consisted of two very sharp and narrow sections, even when the distance between the two-point stimuli, is inside the width of the Mach band type of inhibition, the reduction in sensation magnitude is quite small. If we increase the distance between the two-point stimuli so that the Hering-type of inhibition is involved, then there is almost no inhibitory effect between the two-point stimuli present [pp. 1495–1496].

Second, tachistoscopic exposures (dots last at most for 50 μsec with the P-15 short-persistence phosphor) do not allow sufficient time for the elicitation of the retinal lateral inhibitory mechanisms. This observation has been supported both neurophysiologically (Barlow, Fitzhugh, & Kuffler, 1957) and psychophysically (Nachmias, 1967).

5. Dot-masking procedures provide one of the few ways to continuously vary the recognizability of a form without varying any parameters of the physical stimulus, for example, blur, brightness, or duration of exposure. If the number of dots or the temporal relations between dots of the noise and dots of the signal is varied, it is possible to mix together controlled amounts of signal and noise in a way that allows continuous control of the detectability of a form from levels at which it rarely, if ever, is detected to levels at which it is always correctly detected.

6. It seems also that dot patterns may be more closely analogous than continuous figures are to the way in which nervous signals encode geometry. Nervous signals generated by visual stimuli are mosaiclike, spatial–temporal patterns and, at some neural levels at least, they are conveyed along parallel communication lines by impulsive neural representations. This statement is an oversimplification, of course; it ignores all of the intensive, qualitative, and temporal dimensions of coding. In the present context of form recognition, however, it is intended that these dimensions be ignored. Our emphasis, instead, is on the capabilities of the human visual system to process two-dimensional spatial information.

In sum, dot masking permits examination of a relatively pure form of what is presumably a central visual pattern detection process, separate from the confounding effects of such peripheral variables as photochemistry and lateral neural interactions between contours. It may also be distinguished from other central effects, such as categorization and classification processes. This technique, therefore, allows us to concentrate attention exclusively on the organizational properties of forms composed of dots, each of which possesses identical temporal, intensive, and spatial properties.

II. SOME EXPERIMENTAL STUDIES

A. Introduction

The results of a group of experiments dealing with the detection of dotted geometric forms in dotted visual noise are now reported. Note that Experiments I–VI deal with the detection of dotted lines, whereas

Experiments VII–XI deal with the detection of dotted polygons. One, Experiment XII, was designed specifically to answer the question of the centrality or peripheralness of the masking process, in other words, to determine the locus of the effect. The purpose of this series of experiments was to demonstrate which features of organized forms are important in dot-pattern detection in order to provide an empirical basis for testing a theoretical model based on autocorrelation principles.

B. Experiment I: Effect of Dot Numerosity on Line Detection

What are the basic variables that determine whether a dotted straight line is detected in dotted visual noise? In an earlier study (Uttal, Bunnell, & Corwin, 1970), it was determined that one very strong effect was exerted by variations in interdot spacing. Specifically, closely spaced dots produced figures that were highly resistant to masking, whereas sparsely spaced dots produced figures that were more easily masked. The results of this experiment are shown in Figure 2.3.

The effect of dot numerosity on detectability of lines was also considered in a preliminary experiment of the present study. Clearly, pattern detectability increases as the number of dots in a pattern increases when the number of dots is small (that is, fewer than five). However, two attempts to examine the role of dot numerosity produced conflicting results concerning the existence of a possible asymptote when the number of dots exceeded five or six.

In the first study (Uttal *et al.*, 1970), which used an identification task instead of a detection task and a form of dotted visual noise in which the masking dots were distributed in time, it was observed that an increase in performance occurred for increases in dot numerosity, but only up to about five dots. Beyond five dots, no further advantage appeared to be gained by simply adding dots. However, in another closely related study, using a psychophysical procedure more like the detection paradigm used in the present work (Chinnis & Uttal, 1974), it was observed that detectability increased monotonically with dot numerosity. In fact, if the signal detection measure d' was used instead of the raw percent correct score, the effect appeared to be nearly linear along the d' dimension. Experiment I was an attempt to resolve this dilemma by a third replication.

II. SOME EXPERIMENTAL STUDIES

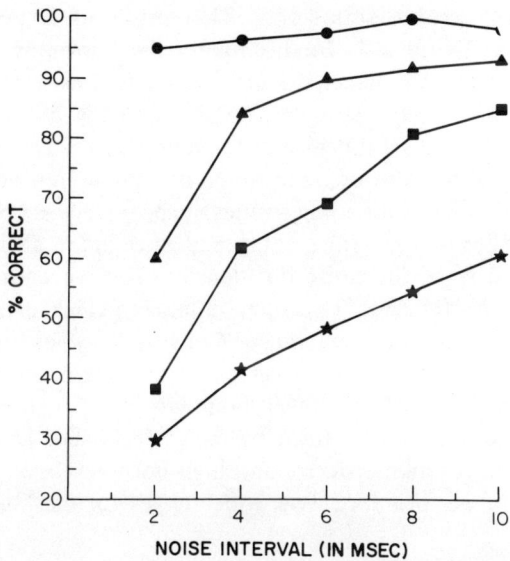

FIGURE 2-3 Graph showing the effect of dot spacing on the detectability of straight lines. The closer the dots, the higher the line detectability. Dot spacing: (●) 17.5′; (▲) 35′; (■) 52.5′; (★) 70′. The data are parametric with spacing between dots (in minutes of visual angle). The horizontal axis indicates intervals between temporally distributed masking dots (an exception in this case).

1. **Stimuli.** A set of 24 dotted-line stimuli were used: four lines consisted of three dots; four of four dots; four of five; four of six; four of seven; and four lines consisted of nine dots. Beyond this maximum numerosity, the number of dots produced stimuli that extended beyond the constrained visual field defined in this experiment, because the interdot spacing in all cases was 38′. One dotted line in each set of four with a given numerosity was oriented vertically; one, horizontally; one, right oblique; and one, left oblique, in order to maintain uncertainty about the line position and thereby to prevent partial cues from signaling the presence of a line. Masking densities of 20, 30, 40, 50, 60, 70, 80, 90, and 100 dcts were used to determine whether any variation in the results was produced as a function of the noise level that could account for the earlier discrepancies.

2. Results and discussion. The results of Experiment I are displayed in Figure 2-4. In this figure, the percentage of the total number of correctly detected stimuli is plotted as a function of the number of dots in the straight line. A family of curves is obtained that is parametric as a function of the number of masking dots. These data display a mixture of three different response curve shapes. For the lines with high dot numerosities, a positively accelerated curve is obtained because the lines composed of dots are all highly detectable, regardless of the noise dot density. This, of course, is a clear example of a "topping" or upper boundary effect caused by a restricted response dimension range. Conversely, when the number of dots in a line is small, the curves are negatively accelerated. This is clearly a "bottoming" or lower boundary effect caused by the response range being constrained by the 50% chance level as a lower bound. Small dot numerosities and high noise levels combine to give low levels of performance over wide ranges for the lines with fewer dots.

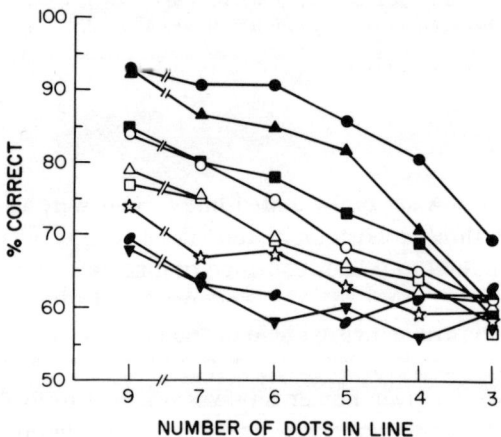

FIGURE 2-4 Graph showing the effect of the number of dots on the detectability of straight lines. The greater the number of dots, the higher the line detectability. Masking dot density: (●) 20; (▲) 30; (■) 40; (○) 50; (△) 60; (□) 70; (☆) 80; (◆) 90; (▼) 100.

However, there is little evidence of any asymptote for the intermediate dot numerosities not constrained by these confounding boundary conditions. There appears to be an almost linear increase in detectability with increases in numerosity over the full range of masking dot densities for intermediate noise dot densities. It seems certain that at some higher numerosities there must be such an asymptote, because the integrative processes that allow individual dots to interact with each other must themselves be limited to some maximum visual angle. If so, it exists outside the range of numerosities used in this experiment.

The conclusion, that increases in dot numerosity continuously improve detection, is valid only for the intermediate value of dot spacings used in this experiment. At smaller dot spacings, the detectability of a stimulus line is very high with even the smallest numerosities; it can be expected to wash out the less robust effect of simple numerosity. When widely spaced, however, dots move out of the region in which a pattern is defined.

C. Experiment II:
The Effect of Orientation on Line Detection

A recent comprehensive review by Appelle (1972) considered the wide variety of visual situations in which some effect of stimulus orientation on vision in animals and humans has been observed. Orientation effects can be very large with some kinds of stimuli and with some tasks. For example, Kolers and Perkins (1969a, b) have shown that the normal orientation of highly overlearned stimulus materials (for example, typed alphabetic characters) is critical to their recognition. Weintraub and Krantz (1971) and others (see Appelle, 1972) have shown variations of an order of magnitude in the Poggendorf illusion, depending on the orientation of the pattern. For another example, Kitterle (1973) has shown that even the ubiquitous simultaneous brightness contrast effect depends to a substantial degree on the orientation of the stimulus pattern. Besides demonstrating the orientation sensitivity of this effect, Kitterle's finding also strongly suggests a central nervous system locus of this illusion.

Such large effects of orientation are most often encountered in situations that make demands on the subject's cognitive information processing at symbolically encoded levels, or they involve illusory stimuli that produce responses which are discrepant with the geometry of the stimuli. Despite repeated suggestions that such illusions may be mediated by some sort of relatively peripheral neural net processing of the original geometric relationships, evidently the cues involved in the production of these illusions have long since been converted or encoded into representations in which the geometry is of secondary importance. It is at this encoded level that orientation effects seem more likely to be produced.

There is also a wide variety of other psychophysical observations in which orientation of the stimulus produces less powerful, but quite significant, differences that apparently have little to do with the cognitive significance or degree of learning of the stimulus set. For example, Campbell, Kulikowski, and Levinson (1966) studied the changes in the resolution of spatial frequencies as a function of orientation of bar patterns, generated directly on the retina by a laser, and found a maximum orientation effect of about 12% of the maximum sensitivity. Many similar examples make it clear that several different orientation effects may be present. What is the influence of orientation must therefore be asked specifically for each task and stimulus set. The purpose of Experiment II, then, was to determine whether or not there was an orientation effect for dotted lines in the masking detection task used in the present study.

1. Stimuli. The stimuli consisted of a set of eight dotted lines. Four of these lines were composed of seven dots with a constant interdot spacing of 40'. The remaining four lines were composed of five dots with the same interdot spacing. Each of the two sets of four lines contained a horizontal, a vertical, a left oblique (315°), and a right oblique (45°) line. The use of four different orientations in this experiment served a dual role. Not only was orientation the major independent variable, but it also provided a means of introducing uncertainty in the subjects about stimulus orientation, thereby helping to reduce the effect of artifacts caused by partial cues. Masking noise densities of 40, 60, 80, 100, 120, 140, and 160 dots were used to produce a parametric family of response curves.

2. Results and discussion. The results for the seven- and five-dot line patterns are plotted in Figures 2-5 and 2-6. Formal tests of significance, as well as direct observation, make it clear that the

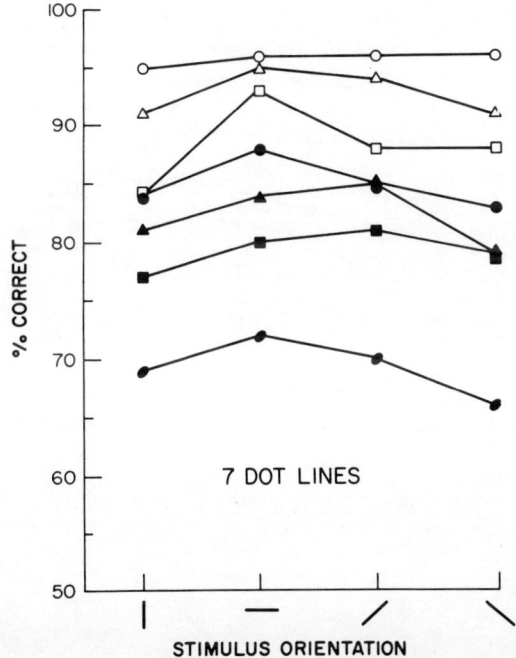

FIGURE 2-5 Graph showing the absence of any effect of line orientation on detectability for lines composed of seven dots. Masking dot density: (○) 40; (△) 60; (□) 80; (●) 100; (▲) 120; (■) 140; (⬗) 160.

dot pattern detection task is insensitive to the orientation of stimulus lines. This finding is contrary both to those very large effects observed in the more complex reading and illusion tasks mentioned above and to the other, less robust effects more often attributed to anisotropies in the optical elements or neural circuits mediating vision. The reason for this difference in sensitivity between our experimental task and the more common findings cannot be immediately identified, but a conjecture is that it may be related to the lack of continuous contours as well as to the way in which subjects initially learn to deal with these relatively novel stimulus sets. This seems to be a reasonable speculation. Except for those secondary factors of resolution and differential sensitivity that can vary with retinal locus, the actual orientations of the dotted lines in our stimuli do not in fact exist, except in an organizational sense, any more than the "lines" themselves exist.

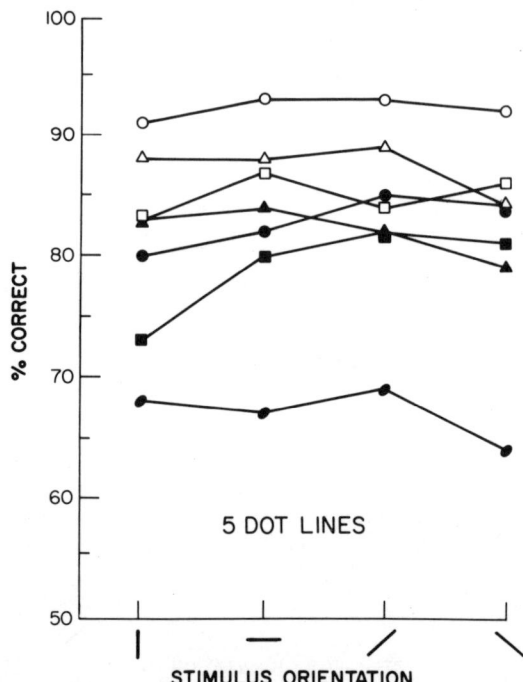

FIGURE 2-6 Graph showing the absence of any effect of line orientation on detectability for lines composed of five dots. Masking dot density: (○) 40; (△) 60; (□) 80; (●) 100; (▲) 120; (■) 140; (⬤) 160.

Therefore, assuming that the dots are seen, they should be equally capable of leading to the inference of a dotted straight line whether they are obliquely or vertically arranged. Empirically, this appears to be the case.

D. Experiment III: The Effect of Curvature and Angulature on Line Detection*

Next to be considered is an important question concerning straight-line detectability. As a result of the recent neurophysiological findings

---

* An expanded version of this section was published previously. See Uttal (1973b).

about cellular sensitivity to oriented straight lines, considerable attention has been directed to perceptual processing of straight lines. There is a widely accepted notion that straight lines are in some way more fundamental in perception that curves or angles. Indeed, earlier psychophysical studies have shown that straight-line components are especially significant in determining the recognizability of alphabetic characters (Uttal, 1969), geometric forms (Uttal, 1971), and even in judgments of figural goodness (Garner & Clement, 1963). In fact, however, little empirical evidence supports the consensus concerning the primacy of straight lines with regard to their own detectability. The question therefore arises: are separate straight lines more easily detected than curves or angles with identical local geometry when assayed by the procedure of this present study?

Experiment III sought to determine the effect on detectability of changes in curvature and angulature for curves and angles of two different sizes. It therefore consists of four parts.

1. Stimuli. The general procedure described above was common to the four parts of this experiment, but different stimulus sets were used: in Parts 1 and 2, straight lines were deformed into curves; in Parts 3 and 4, straight lines were deformed into angles. Each stimulus set contained six sequential steps of increasing curvature or angulature for each of four different initial straight line orientations—a total of 24 different stimuli—in order to maintain the subject's uncertainty about specific dot locations.

A sample of each of the four stimulus sets is shown in Figure 2-7. In each case, the six (of 24) stimuli produced by the downward deformation of a horizontal line were chosen as the sample; in other instances, the orientation of the initial lines was vertical or oblique in either the left or right direction.

Part 1 of this experiment utilized curvature—specifically, a line of nine dots separated by 33' of visual angle, producing a total line length of 4° 24'. The stepwise increase in curvature shown in Figure 2-7 was arbitrarily determined for successive stimuli. Because earlier work (Uttal, Bunnell, & Corwin, 1970) had shown that the spacing of dots in straight lines was a powerful determinant of their detectability and recognizability, a family of curves in which dots were less densely placed was used in Part 2 in order to examine the effects

48 2. THE PSYCHOPHYSICAL EXPERIMENTS

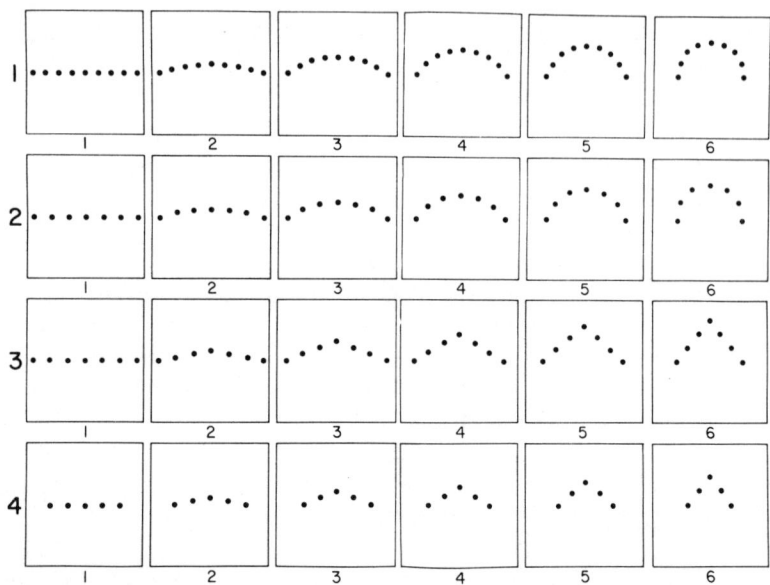

FIGURE 2-7 Sample target patterns used in the experiment determining the effect of the angulature or curvature of a line on its detectability.

of that variable. A line of seven dots, 4° 24′ in length, was used in this phase, defining an interdot interval of 44′ of visual angle.

In Parts 3 and 4, straight lines were progressively deformed into more acute angles. The increasing angulature was in 20° steps from 180° (a straight line) to an 80° angle. Because it is known that the detectability of straight lines is influenced by the number of dots in the line (compare with Experiment I), the stimuli in Parts 3 and 4 were composed of lines and angles that included seven and five dots, respectively, spaced 44′ apart in each case, for a total line length of 4° 34′ and 3° 6′.

Within each of the four parts of the experiment the local properties consisting of interdot spacing, total length, and number of dots remained constant. Only the global pattern was varied.

2. Results and discussion. The results for the four parts of the experiment are shown in Figures 2-8, 2-9, 2-10, and 2-11. In each figure, the percentage of the total number of correctly detected

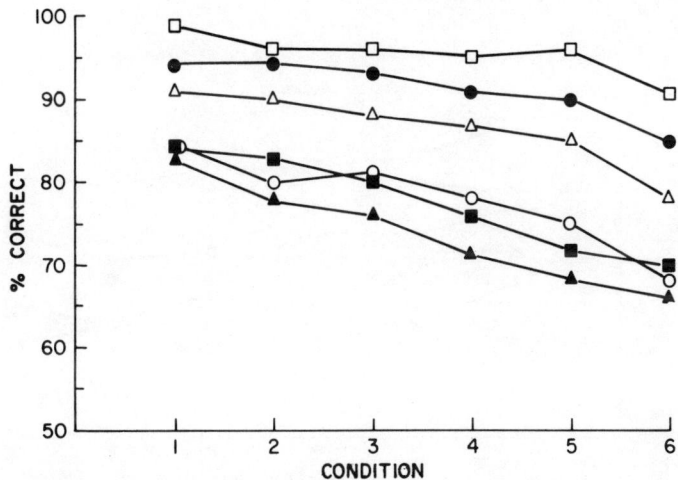

FIGURE 2-8 Graph showing the effect of curvature on a nine-dot line. The greater the curvature, the less the detectability. Masking dot density: (□) 60; (●) 80; (△) 100; (■) 120; (○) 140; (▲) 160. (From Uttal, 1973b.)

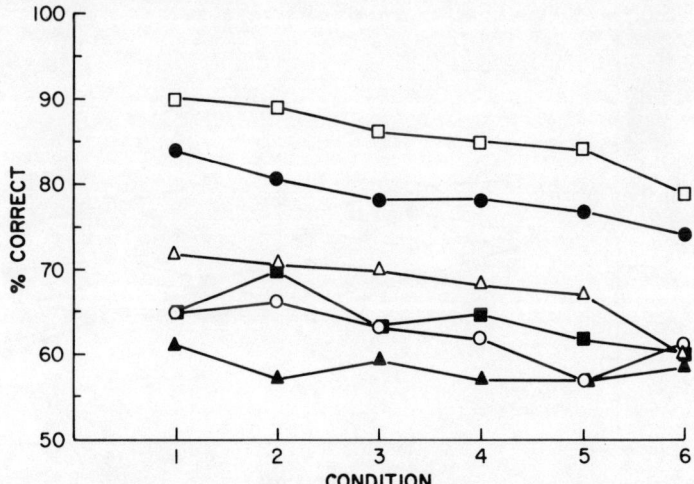

FIGURE 2-9 Graph showing the effect of curvature on a seven-dot line. The greater the curvature, the less the detectability. Masking dot density: (□) 60; (●) 80; (△) 100; (■) 120; (○) 140; (▲) 160. (From Uttal, 1973b.)

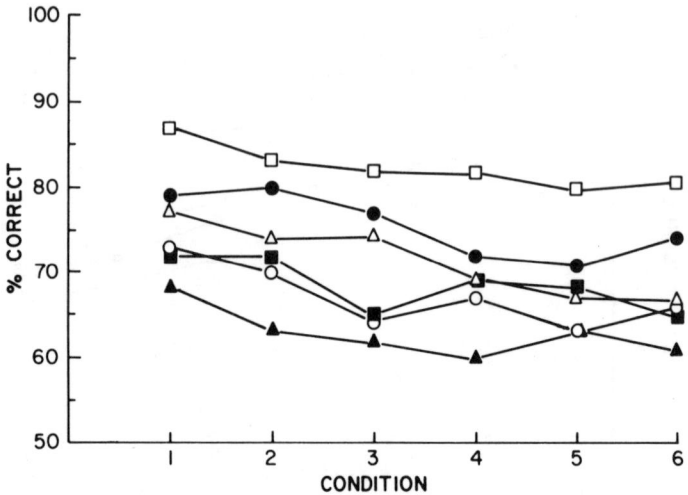

FIGURE 2-10 Graph showing the effect of angulature on a seven-dot line. The greater the angulature, the less the detectability. Masking dot density: (□) 60; (●) 80; (△) 100; (■) 120; (○) 140; (▲) 160. (From Uttal, 1973b.)

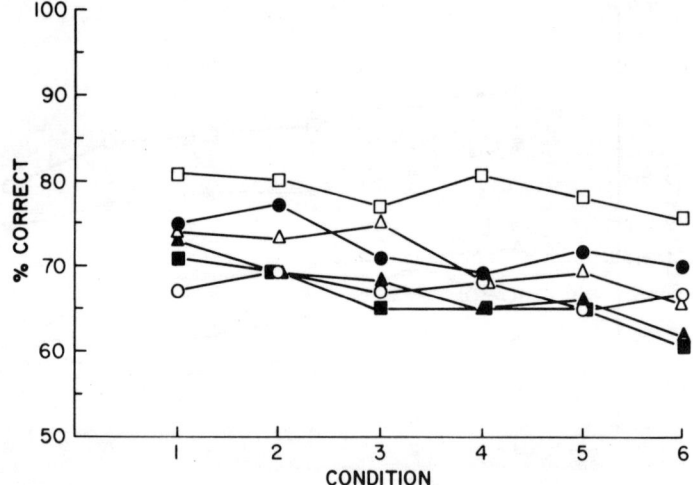

FIGURE 2-11 Graph showing the effect of angulature on a five-dot line. The greater the angulature, the less the detectability. Masking dot density: (□) 60; (●) 80; (△) 100; (■) 120; (○) 140; (▲) 160. (From Uttal, 1973b.)

stimuli is plotted as a function of the degree of curvature or angulature parametrically for the various noise levels. The pooled data are given in Table 2-1. The major finding is apparent: there is a gradual decline in the detectability of the line as deviation from linearity increases. The decline is most pronounced for the large curves of Part 1, because of their higher absolute level of detectability, but is also present to a lesser extent in Parts 2, 3, and 4. There is, however, little indication that the decrease in detectability is sensitive in any strongly nonlinear manner to the increase in either curvature or angulature. There is no discontinuity or point of inflection on any of the curves, a finding that seems to provide at least circumstantial support for the notion that no separate or distinct mechanisms are being called into play at different levels of geometrical deformation. Such a linear and continuous process is further indicated by the general parallel course of the family of curves in each figure. The only notable exception to this generalization is a slight increase in spread as one passes from the data for the straight line to those for the curves.

Comparisons between Parts 1 and 2 do show one expected difference. The absolute level of detectability of the more densely plotted dots in Part 1 is greater than the less densely plotted dots of Part 2.

Table 2-1 also underscores another point. Allowing for the general decline in performance as angulature and curvature increase, there

TABLE 2-1
Decline in Detectability as a Function of Increasing Angulature or Curvature for the Four Parts of Experiment III Pooled across All Noise Levels

Part	Condition (as shown in Fig. 2-7)					
	1	2	3	4	5	6
1	89	86.8	85.6	83	81	76.3
2	72.8	72.3	69.8	69	67.6	65.3
3	76	73	70.7	69.8	69.3	69
4	73.5	72.8	70.5	69.3	69.2	67.0

is little further difference between equivalent conditions of Parts 2, 3, and 4 for which the dot spacing is constant. Again, dot spacing can be seen to play the most important role in determining the detectability of these patterns. Other variables seem to be less influential in their effect on detectability.

The main question raised by these findings is why are straight lines more easily detected than curves or angles when local properties are held constant? An explanation based on template matching or specific feature filtering leaves many unresolved problems. For example, it is necessary to explain the origin of sensitivity to specific forms. From a perspective involving templates, one is also hard pressed to explain how a figure belonging to some general class but that itself has not yet been seen, or has not yet been seen in a specific orientation, can be recognized as easily as a familiar figure in a familiar orientation. All template models of visual pattern perception, whether based on single or multicellular premises, fall victim to this criticism. Furthermore, template theories do not adequately model the insensitivity to magnification, rotation, and translation, all of which seem to characterize the recognition of dotted stimuli.

Clearly, some form recognition process, sensitive to global rather than to local features and not requiring an internally stored template, is called for. An autocorrelation model that exhibits many of the requisite properties is presented in Chapter 3.

E. Experiment IV: The Effect of Irregular Spacing on Collinear Dotted-Line Detection*

A parameter of particular interest to this study is the regularity of dot spacing in a straight dotted line. An experiment exploring this parameter was reported earlier as part of a longer study by Chinnis and Uttal (1974) but, because of its special importance, the results of that experiment are reconsidered briefly at this point.

Consider for a moment the question of how a straight line of dots differs from an equivalent number of randomly placed noise dots. There are, in fact, only two organizational cues that can be used to

* Adapted from Chinnis and Uttal (1975).

II. SOME EXPERIMENTAL STUDIES

distinguish a straight-line signal from the noise dots. The first one is the collinearity of the dots: the dots of the signal are arranged along the axis of the line, in a way that helps the observer to detect their organization and distinctiveness from the visual noise. The other way in which a straight line varies from noise is the regularity of the spacing of the dots along this line. The next experiment to be discussed deals with this problem of collinearity by examining the effect of perturbations in the position of the dots perpendicular to the axis of the line. First, however, an experiment concerning the effects of perturbations in the regularity of the spacing of the dots along the straight line, but with maintained collinearity, is examined.

1. Stimuli. Dotted-line stimuli with varying degrees of spacing irregularity oriented either horizontally or vertically were used in this experiment. Here the subject's task was simply to specify the orientation of the line of dots presented in a single stimulus burst, and not to select in which of a pair of stimulus bursts the line occurred as was required in most of the other experiments in this study.

The set of stimuli used varied in terms of the spacing irregularity between a variable number of linearly arrayed dots. As few as three or as many as seven dots could be present in the line. The equally spaced, prototypical lines had interdot spacings of 45' of visual angle. This regular spacing then was perturbed by randomly adding 4.5' or to subtracting 4.5' from the regular spacing between each pair of dots (along the axis of the line) a variable number of times. An arbitrary selection of the number of times (R) that this addition or subtraction occurred for each trial allowed a subjectively smooth transition from perfectly regular to seemingly random spacing. The arbitrary perturbation values chosen were $R = 0, 2, 7, 14,$ and 56.

A sample of nine stimulus patterns embedded in a constant amount of dotted noise is shown in Figure 2-12 for three R values and for three dot numerosities. Note in this figure that each line with a given number of dots is equal in length to every other line with that same numerosity. The average interdot spacing is therefore also equal in each line, regardless of R, for constant dot numerosity.

Following the perturbing additions and subtractions, the entire line was restored to its original length by multiplying it by a constant and by then laterally displacing it in a random direction by, at most,

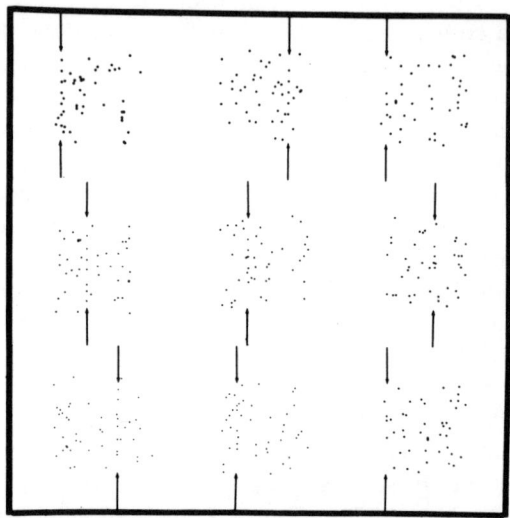

FIGURE 2-12 Sample stimuli, containing both targets and noise, from the experiment in which spacing irregularity and number of dots were varied. Vertical columns have seven, five, and three dots, respectively, in each target. Horizontal rows have variability indices (R_n) ranging from perfectly regular at the top, to moderately irregular, to very irregular at the bottom. Arrows indicate locations of stimuli. (From Chinnis & Uttal, 1975.)

25′ of visual angle to reduce the contribution of partial cues. Individual dots in a line were constrained from being closer than 5′ to avoid fusion and therefore discrimination on the basis of brightness differences. The number of noise dots was held constant at 40 in this experiment.

2. Results and discussion. Results are displayed in Figure 2-13, with the usual response measure (percentage correct) plotted as a function of the number of dots in the signal line. A family of curves is produced by varying the parameter of interdot spacing irregularity.

Two notable effects are apparent in this data. First, there is a regular, monotonic increase in the detectability of the line as a function of the number of dots, confirming the findings in Experiment I above. Second, there is a regular, monotonic decrease in the detectability of the line as the irregularity in dot spacing increases (as indicated

II. SOME EXPERIMENTAL STUDIES

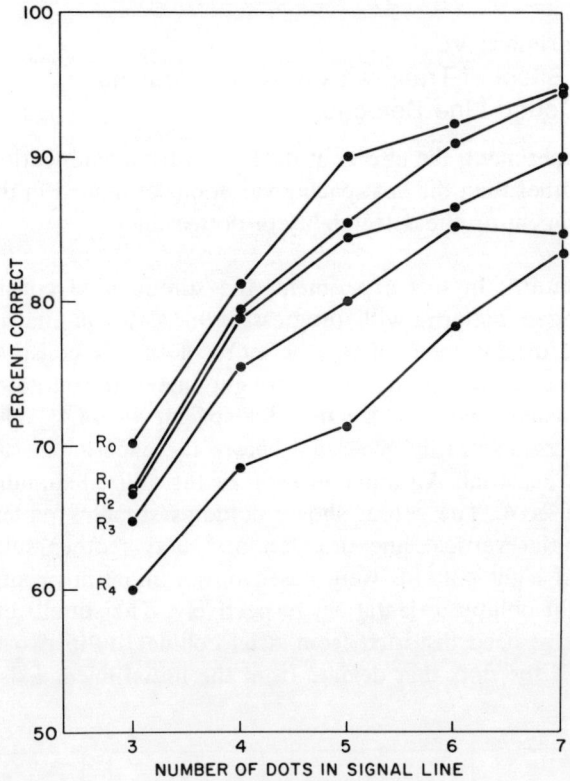

FIGURE 2-13 Graph showing the effects of variation in the regularity (R_n) of dot spacing on detectability of straight lines composed of 3, 4, 5, 6, and 7 dots, respectively. The more irregular the spacing, the less the detectability of the line. (From Chinnis & Uttal, 1975.)

by the R value). The absolute amount of this difference is substantial and can be seen to be as large as 20 percentage points (i.e., greater than 40% of the total possible performance range) at a numerosity of five dots. Therefore, we may conclude that the regularity of spacing of a collinear array of dots plays a significant role in the detectability of the line in random dotted noise. This result played a major role in selecting the autocorrelation function as a model of this type of form detection. It is well known that the autocorrelation transform is especially sensitive to periodicities in the pattern being processed.

F. Experiment V: The Effect of Transverse Irregular Spacing on Dotted-Line Detection

In this experiment, the effects of deviations from collinearity are considered rather than the dot spacing variations examined in the preceding experiment on the detectability of dotted lines.

1. Stimuli. In this experiment, the stimuli used consisted of a set of dotted patterns with progressive increases in the amount of transverse displacement of one or more of the six constituent dots. The prototypical pattern was a straight line with a total length of 3.7° of visual angle and an interdot spacing of 44.4'. The various stimuli were arbitrarily generated before the experiment rather than anew on each trial. A sample of eight of the utilized stimuli is shown in Figure 2-14. The subset shown contains stimulus patterns based on an initial vertical line orientation; the two other subsets (not shown) of eight patterns were based on an initial horizontal and an initial right oblique orientation, respectively. The stimuli in all three subsets have been distorted from strict collinearity in two ways: the number of the dots that deviate from the initial linear axis is varied

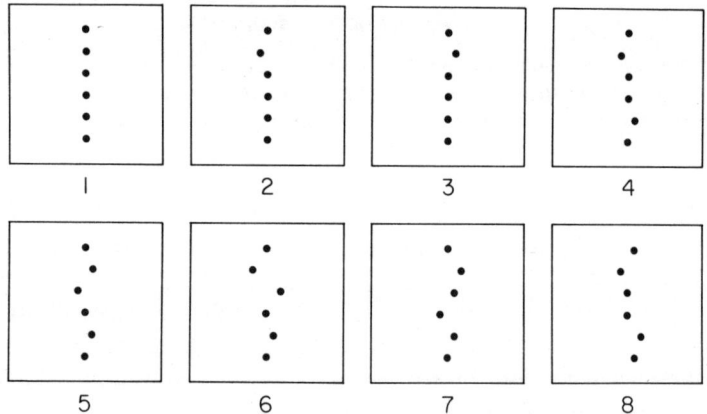

FIGURE 2-14 Sample target patterns used in the experiment determining the effect of transverse irregularity on line detection.

and so is the magnitude of the deviation for each displaced dot. An index of the degree of deviation can, therefore, be computed for each stimulus pattern:

$$D = \sum_{i=0}^{n} d, \qquad (2\text{-}1)$$

where D is the index of deviation and d is the deviation in degrees of visual angle from the axis of collinearity for each of n displaced dots.

In this experiment, the design reverted to the standard two-alternative, forced-choice procedure used in most of the other experiments in this study. Noise densities of 0, 10, 20, 30, and 40 randomly placed dots were used to scan the masking range, to determine whether there were any differences in the effect of transverse spacing as a function of detection task difficulty.

2. Results and discussion. The results of the experiment are shown in Figure 2-15. The percentages of correct detections have been plotted as a function of the indices of deviation from Eq. (2-1) for each of the eight types of stimuli. Clearly, the simple deviation score used was not a perfect predictor of the obtained result—the obtained curve is not entirely monotonic. Stimuli 3 and 6 received a somewhat lower detection score than would be predicted if this simple deviation index accounted for all of the variance. However, the overall pattern of the results is unambiguous. There is a gradual decline in the detectability of the patterns from the regular line (Stimulus 1) as the pattern becomes less regular at all masking dot densities. This difference is about 15% of detection scores, a value equivalent to a variation of 30% of the total possible response range. Although the actual dimensions that have been varied in both the present experiment and the previous experiment (in which dotted collinear lines varied in spacing irregularity) are not directly comparable in both experiments, and although different groups of subjects have been used, it is interesting to note that the variation in detectability scores is approximately the same for the two experiments.

Therefore, we may conclude that transverse displacement from regular straightness also plays a significant role in reducing the detectability of lines, although the lack of a monotonic function suggests

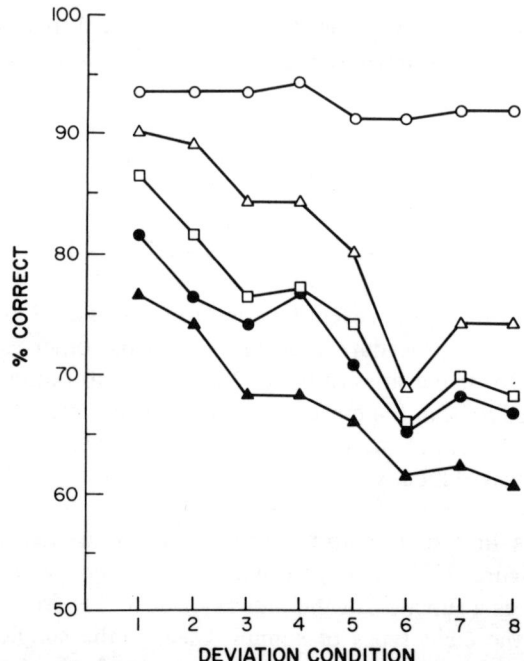

FIGURE 2-15 Graph showing the effects of transverse irregularity on the detectability of straight lines. The greater the transverse irregularity, the less the detectability of the line. Masking dot density: (○) 0; (△) 10; (□) 20; (●) 30; (▲) 40.

that the index of deviation is only part of the story. Other factors, such as the "symmetry" of the perturbed pattern, probably also play a role in determining the detectability of these dotted stimulus patterns.

G. Experiment VI: Critical Parts in Triangle Recognition*

This experiment also was reported more fully in another publication (Uttal, 1971), but because of its particular relevance and the germinal role it played in setting the stage for the later studies of dotted polygon detection, it is briefly reviewed at this point. The question

---

* Adapted from Uttal (1971).

posed was: What parts of a dotted triangle—the sides or the corners—are most decisive in determining its detectability when it is masked by random visual noise dots? To answer this question, triangles with missing parts were presented and the detectability of each type of triangle was determined by a procedure in which the subject was required simply to specify the orientation of the triangle. The triangle might have its apex pointing to the left, right, up, or down. A comparison was made of the effects on recognizability of deleting dots from the corners, from the sides, or a random selection of dots from any part of the triangle. Visual noise was presented as a 2-sec sequence of randomly positioned dots separated by 8, 6, 4, 3, 2, and 1 μsec. This dynamic noise, which was perceptually unlike the burst of dots used in most of the other experiments of this study, increased in apparent density with decreases in the interval between the noise dots.

1. Stimuli. The five types of stimulus patterns used are shown in Figure 2-16, which displays the triangles for the upward orientation only. Fifteen other triangles, oriented downwards (five), to the left (five), and to the right (five) were also used. Stimuli of Type I were complete shapes with nine dots on each side. Type II omitted the three dots at each of the corners, Type III omitted the three center dots on each side. Type IV stimuli omitted the five dots at each of the corners. Type V was a configuration in which random patterns of nine dots were dropped from all parts of the triangle. For a Type V triangle, the selection of the randomly dropped points was made just before the triangle was presented but no record was kept of the specific form of the randomly mutilated stimuli. A single triangle was randomly selected from among the 20 different stimuli for presentation in each trial.

2. Results and discussion. Figure 2-17 displays the data as a function of the noise level, with the data factored on the basis of the five types of displayed triangles. The results of this analysis indicate that the deletion of the three dots at each angle of the triangle caused almost exactly the same modest decrement in recognizability as did the random deletion of nine dots from the figure. On the other hand, the deletion of three dots from the center of the line, thus diminishing the long straight lines of the sides, resulted in a significantly

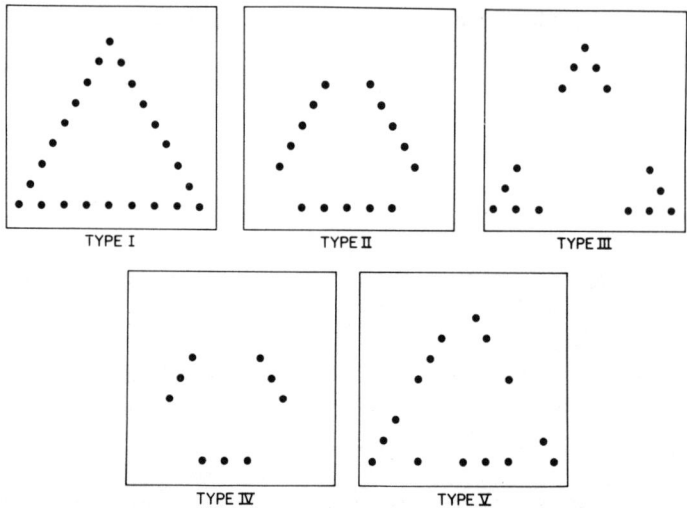

FIGURE 2-16 Samples of the five types of target patterns used in the experiment determining the effect on detectability of mutilating dotted triangles. The same stimuli were also used in three other orientations (apex down, to the right, or to the left).

greater decrease. Even more damaging to the recognizability of the character was the deletion of all but three of the side dots, as might have been anticipated.

The first interpretation that might be presented as an explanation of these data is this: the sides of the dotted triangle and the relationships among them are the most salient features affecting the recognizability of triangles. This theory suggests that the corners themselves have no more influence on the recognition of the character than does the deletion of an equal number of random dots. This notion would be in substantial disagreement with the fact that the information content of the corner dots is greater than that of the side dots. Information theoretical measures would predict a richness of significance, or, more formally, of "information," of the dots of the corner regions because at the corners the redundancy of each part of the pattern is low, owing to the discontinuities in the direction of the line; each corner dot thus conveys more information.

Although these data show, contrarily, that the recognizability of triangles is more influenced by the component straight line segments than by the component corners, there is a possible alternative expla-

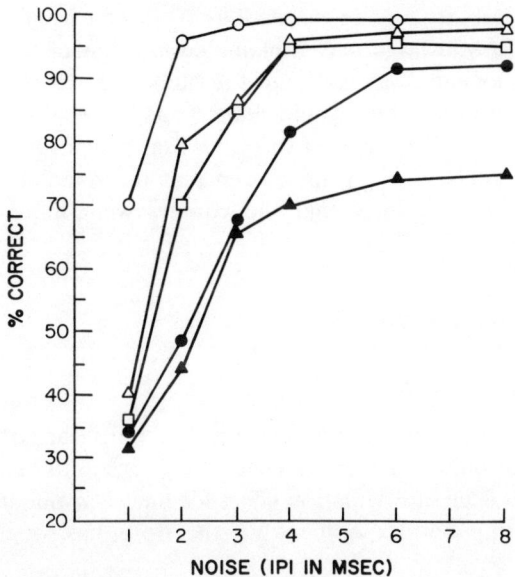

FIGURE 2-17 Graph showing the effect of triangle mutilations on their detectability. Types of mutilation indicated in Fig. 2-16: (○) Type I; (△) Type II; (□) Type V; (●) Type III; (▲) Type IV. Removing corners and random deletions degrades detectability less than does removing sides. This experiment is also exceptional in its use of noise dots temporally distributed in time with the interval indicated.

nation, namely, that, in fact, neither the corners nor the sides are more or less critical to the recognition of the form. What is important is that, in some way, information about the global geometry of the form is presented to the observer. Because we know from Experiment III that the linear sides are more detectable than the angular corners, all other parameters being equal, it may be that the higher detectability of the sides makes triangular forms composed of sides more easily detectable than forms composed of corners. However, in either case, the necessary cue for triangularity is that some kind of information be made available about the global organization of the figure. This information can be presented by using either a side or a corner, just as a "chair" could be recognized when created from almost any type of component part as shown by Koler's chairs. The essential aspect of the process is with regard to that information concerning organization, not to the nature of the parts. In other words, differences in

62 2. THE PSYCHOPHYSICAL EXPERIMENTS

global detectability among the various types of triangles used in this experiment are in large part explainable in terms of the detectability of the components that make up the global forms.

Such an interpretation would make good sense of previously contradictory results. In those experiments that had suggested some primacy for corners, it might have been that the stimulus material was designed in such a way that the corners were more visible than the sides.

H. Experimental VII: The Effect of Rotation on the Detection of Polygons

It is inappropriate to generalize from data on linear stimuli patterns to polygonal ones, for there is no a priori reason to assume that the observed absence of orientation effect for lines is maintained for more complicated figures. Experiment VI, therefore, has sought to answer

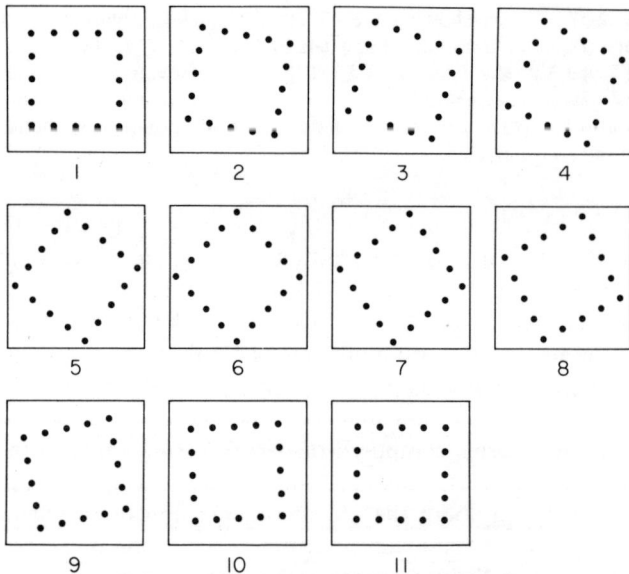

FIGURE 2-18 Sample target patterns used in the experiment determining the effect of rotation of squares on their detectability.

II. SOME EXPERIMENTAL STUDIES

the question of the presence or absence of orientation effects in the recognition of triangles and squares, the two simplest polygons.

1. Stimuli. Dotted triangles and squares composed of dots separated by 41.4′ of visual angle were used as stimuli. Eleven orientations of each pattern were presented. Figure 2-18 shows the set of oriented squares in which each pattern was rotated from its predecessor's position by 9°. Figure 2-19 shows the 11 orientations of the triangles in which each pattern was rotated from its predecessor's position by 12°. One of the set of 22 stimuli was randomly selected by a computer algorithm on each trial and presented in an amount of visual noise that varied each day. The noise levels used were 60, 80, 100, 120, 140, and 160 randomly placed dots.

2. Results and discussion. Results are shown in Figure 2-20 (for the squares) and in Figure 2-21 (for the triangles). In both, the percentage of the total number of stimuli that were correctly detected is plotted as a function of the orientation and noise level. The

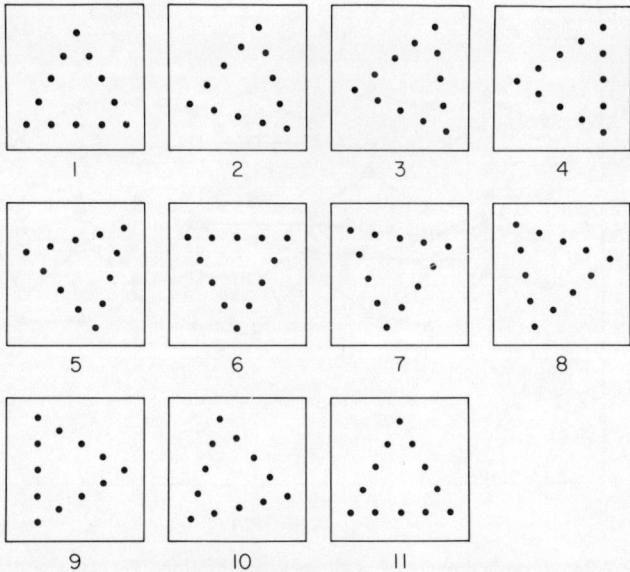

FIGURE 2-19 Sample target patterns used in the experiment determining the effect of rotation of triangles on their detectability.

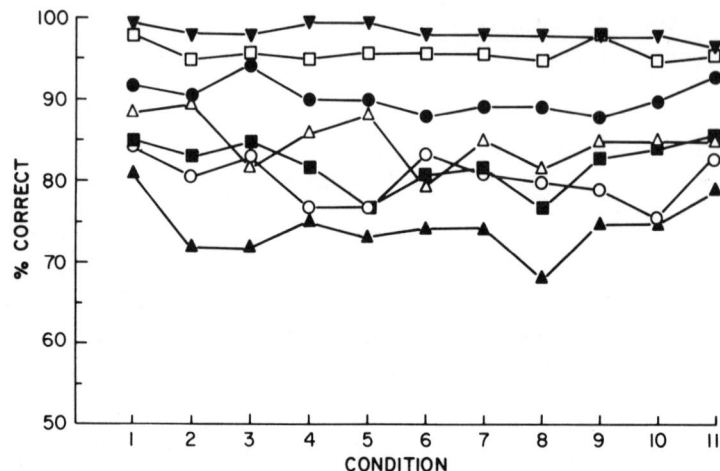

FIGURE 2-20 Graph showing that there is no rotation effect on the detectability of squares. Masking dot density: (▼) 40; (□) 60; (●) 80; (△) 100; (■) 120; (○) 140; (▲) 160.

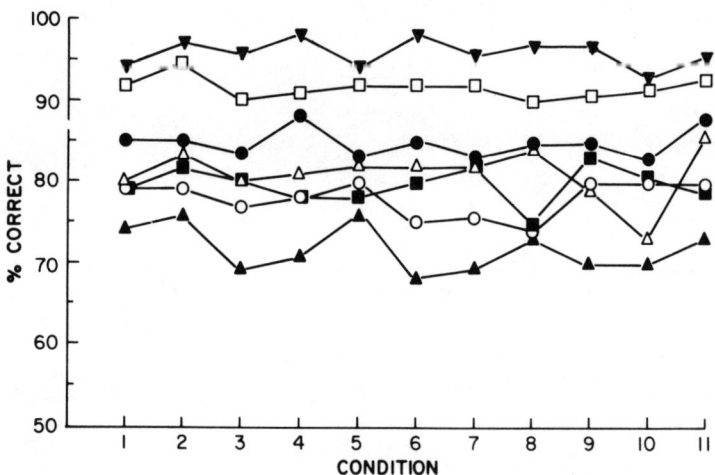

FIGURE 2-21 Graph showing that there is no rotation effect on the detectability of triangles. Masking dot density: (▼) 40; (□) 60; (●) 80; (△) 100; (■) 120; (○) 140; (▲) 160.

general result is, again, that there is little effect of stimulus orientation on the detectability of those dotted polygons. Although this finding is contrary to many findings that do show some orientation effect in other visual perceptual contexts, it is, in retrospect, not too surprising considering the particular class of stimulus material being used in the present experiments. As has been pointed out above, the dots are independent entities, and the patterns they produce (a line, a triangle, a square, etc.) result from their organization into patterns. Yet, the presence of an organized line of dots is not equivalent to the presence of a continuous linear contour. The processing of the individual dots is expected to be isotropic, bounded only by the limitation that their physical properties are above the thresholds determined by retinal locus effects. Given that this threshold is exceeded, the organization of the dot patterns is therefore independent of any anisotropic effects in the retina or at higher levels of the nervous system.

We may therefore conclude that, as with dotted lines, the detection of polygonal patterns is not affected by the orientation of the figure over wide ranges of noise density.

III. SOME EXPERIMENTS ON ORGANIZATION

Let us now turn to a group of experiments that deal with the effect of global pattern organization on the detectability of dotted patterns in dotted noise. These organizational properties are among the ones emphasized by Gestalt psychologists. The various principles of figural goodness and grouping or general organization are too well known, too various, and too often described (as well as being too ambiguous and vague) to require restatement here. The experiments to be described concern only a few of the many properties considered by Gestalt theorists to be effective in determining the visual perceptibility of stimuli.

The major problem with the Gestalt formulation has always been the lack of a quantitative metric for figural "organization." As will be shown, the dot-pattern assay technique offers a direct means of testing stimulus patterns so that they can, at least, be ordered along these dimensions, even if the dimensions cannot be specifically defined.

If one were to seek some general law that is most characteristic of the Gestalt formulation, it would be the "law of Pragnanz"—the notion that perceptions of "form will be as good as they can be under any given stimulus circumstances." A corollary of this law is that "good" forms are seen better than poor forms, and this corollary is the theme tested by many of the remaining experiments to be described in this chapter. In general, our goal is to take a set of component parts and arrange them into forms with differing degrees of order or goodness and compare the effect of these manipulations of global organization of the stimulus on its detectability. To anticipate the findings discussed in this section, it can be said that the results indicate that, although a number of aspects of form do contribute effectively to detection scores, at least one concept of figural goodness, that tested by Garner and Clement (1963), seems not to influence detectability.

A. Experiment VIII:
The Effect of Figural Organization on Dotted-Form Detection

A first experiment to explore the effect of figural organization of dotted polygonal stimuli on detectability in dotted visual noise deals with squares that are distorted in sequential steps into more and more acute parallelograms. The idea that a square is a better figure than an acute parallelogram can be quantified in any number of ways. Information about the nature of a single side is all that is necessary to fully define any square. Similarly, the four angles are all also the same. In information terms, the redundancy of the square can thus be said to be greater than in other four-sided polygons. In Gestalt terms, the figure is "good" because each part, side or angle, is as much like the other corresponding parts as it can be.

This first test of figural goodness therefore explores the effect on detectability as the figural properties change, but in a situation in which the component parts—the four straight lines (the sides) of dots—are constant throughout the entire range of distortion. In addition, spacing between the dots on the sides remains constant at 42.6°

III. SOME EXPERIMENTS ON ORGANIZATION 67

of visual angle. Local geometry is thereby kept constant throughout this experiment.

1. Stimuli. Figure 2-22 shows six of the 24 patterns used in this experiment. The remaining 18 were organized into three equivalent groups except that the distortion was produced by "flexing" the square in another direction in each case. Six were distorted by leaning the figure to the left while keeping the bottom and top of the square aligned along their original axes. The other 12 were distorted upward or downward, keeping the vertical sides aligned along their original axes. This variation in distorting directions and axes helped, as in previous experiments, to provide some uncertainty about the location of specific dots or parts of the figures and, thereby, to insure that the subject was responding on the basis of his perception of the entire pattern and not on some partial cue. Noise dot densities of 60, 80, 100, 120, 140, and 160 dots were used to produce a family of parametric curves as a function of noise density.

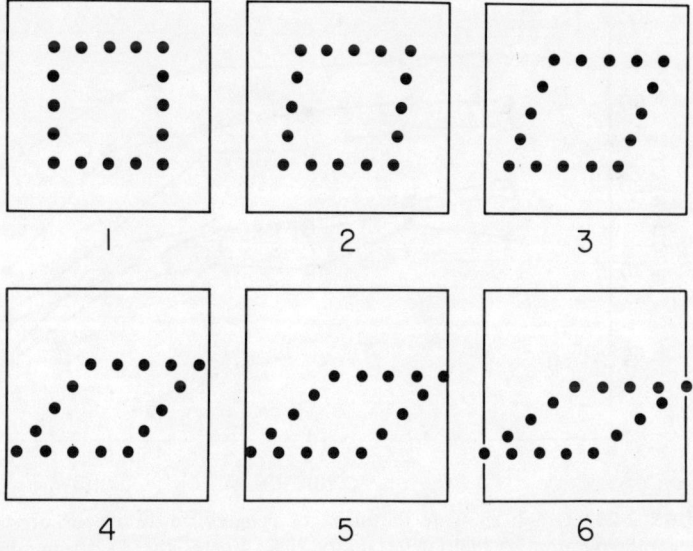

FIGURE 2-22 Sample target patterns used in the experiment determining the effect of the distortion of squares into parallelograms on their detectability.

2. Results. The results are plotted in Figure 2-23. The data have been pooled for all four equivalent conditions from each set of six distorted figures. For example, Condition 6 is the combined result of the four most acute parallelograms from the four sets, regardless of the direction of distortion. Clearly, in spite of the fact that dot spacing has remained constant in the lines and has even increased in density in the general areas of the most acute corners, the effect of the distortion from the square is a reduction in the detectability of the dotted figure in the dotted noise. The typical decrease in the performance score is about 10% from the most regular figure, the square, to the most acute parallelogram. This is not a large amount—only about 20% of the total response range—but it is impressive considering that the physical stimulus energy has remained constant (that is, the dots are always present in equal numbers and of equal brightnesses) and that the local geometry (the nature of the dotted lines that make up the sides) of the figure has also remained constant. Therefore, the effect can only be attributed to the global organization of the component sides.

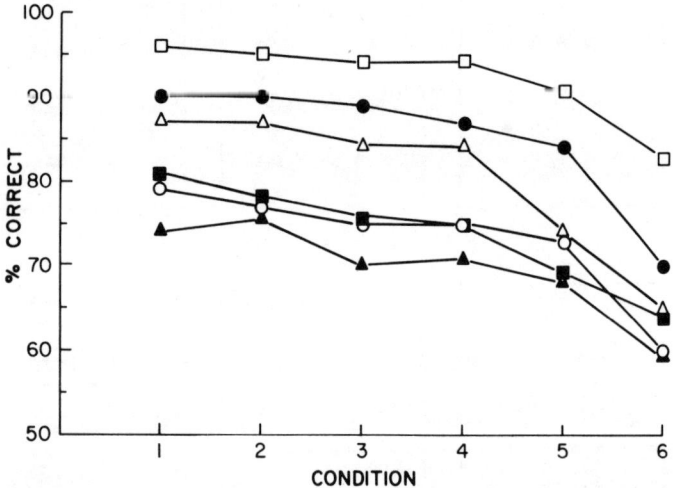

FIGURE 2-23 Graph showing the effect of progressive distortions of squares into parallelograms on their detectability. The greater the distortion, the less the detectability of the target. Masking dot density: (□) 60; (●) 80; (△) 100; (■) 120; (○) 140; (▲) 160.

B. Experiment IX:
Further Effects of Figural Organization

Now that it has been shown that the global organization of the parts of a stimulus can be an influential determinant of the overall detectability of a form, it is necessary to ask whether or not there is something special about that one particularly good and highly symmetrical form, the square, or whether good organization, in general, is the criterion on which the changes in performance are based.

To explore this problem, a two-part experiment was conducted with patterns composed of three and four dotted-line segments, respectively. The main goal was to compare the detectability of several different "good" organizations of two sets of line segments with the detectability of less organized arrangements of the same two sets of segments. This experiment, in addition to the preceding one, served a particularly useful role because it stressed the importance of order per se above and beyond the criterion for detection already imposed by the characteristics of the component line segments themselves. The results strongly supported the idea that the various interactions that could occur between components of a figure transcended the simple dot density and numerosity effects already observed for straight lines. The suggestion that there might be several different kinds of interactions present, including those that occurred between groups of dots as well as those that occurred between individual dots, therefore arose as a direct result of the empirical studies.

1. Stimuli. The stimuli used for the two subexperiments are shown in Figures 2-24 and 2-25. The first set of 12 stimuli (Figure 2-24) was composed of patterns made from three dotted-line segments with three different kinds of organization. The first (Patterns 1–3) are simply "pick-up-sticks," quasi-random patterns. These were chosen by random selection procedures with one constraint: there could be no crossing of any of the line segments, a qualification that also was a characteristic of the ordered stimulus patterns. Three of the figures were triangles (Patterns 4–6), two of which were rotated 90° and 180°, respectively, whereas the other six figures (Patterns 7–12) were arrangements of the three lines in either vertical (Patterns 7–9) or horizontal (Patterns 10–12) parallel formations. In these last

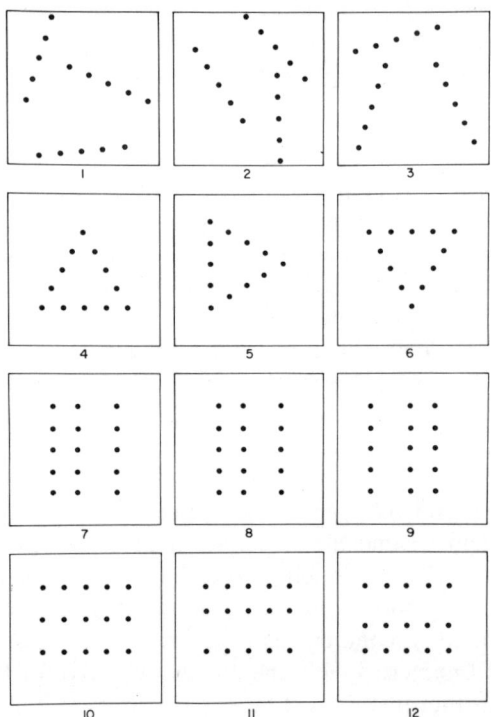

FIGURE 2-24 Sample target patterns from the experiment determining the effect of the degree of organization of three line segments on their detectability.

six patterns, three different conditions of spacing were used; in all cases, however, the average spacing remained constant and so the total size of the figure was constant for all six patterns. The rotated triangles served an additional function as a control for the earlier examination of polygonal rotation (Experiment VII) by embedding these figures in quite a different context than one composed purely of squares.

The 12 patterns of the four line-segment figures, as shown in Figure 2-25, are analogous to the three line patterns used in the first part of the experiment, and the same rationale holds for their selection. Noise levels of 60, 80, 100, 120, 140, and 160 dots were used to produce a parametric family of masking curves for both parts of this experiment.

III. SOME EXPERIMENTS ON ORGANIZATION 71

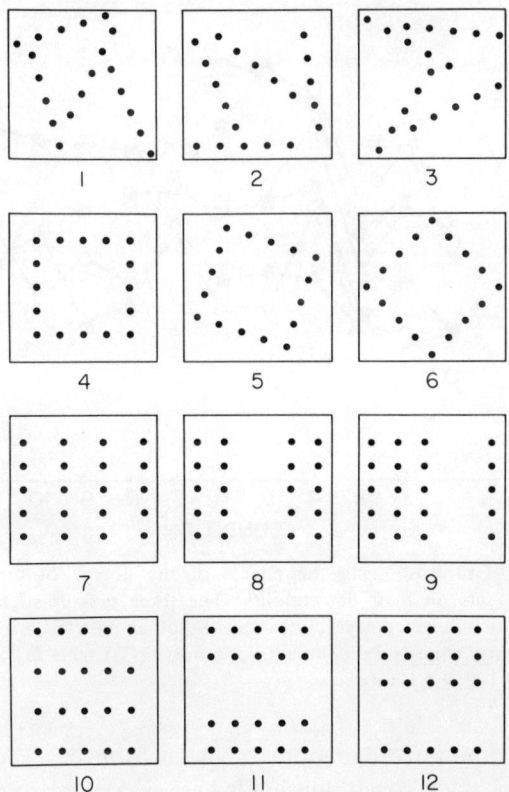

FIGURE 2-25 Sample target patterns from the experiment determining the effect of the degree of organization of four line segments on their detectability.

2. Results and discussion. Results for the four-sided figures are shown in Figure 2-26. The general finding is obvious; there is little difference observed at any noise density level for patterns in which the four line segments are organized into regular patterns. However, two of the three disorganized patterns (Patterns 1 and 3) show a consistent deficit in detectability, whereas the third (Pattern 2) is elevated somewhat above that reduced level. An examination of Pattern 2 indicates that it is moderately symmetrical and therefore spuriously possesses, to a modest degree, some of the organizational properties that enhance the detectability of the more regular patterns.

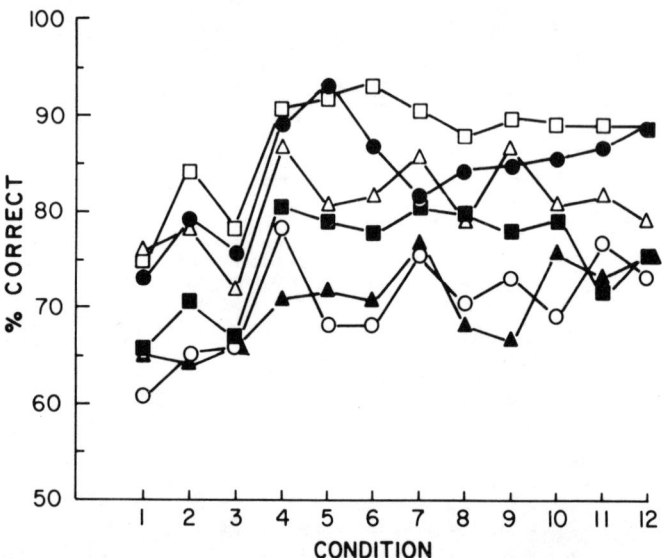

FIGURE 2-26 Graph showing the effects of the degree of organization of three line segments on their detectability. The three pick-up-sticks patterns in Fig. 2-24 display a lower detectability than the other patterns, all of which are organized in some way. Number of masking dots: (□) 60; (●) 80; (△) 100; (■) 120; (○) 140; (▲) 160.

Results for the three dotted-line segment forms are shown in Figure 2-27. The same conclusion holds here in a more robust fashion. Those patterns (Patterns 4–12) composed of regular arrays of the three dotted-line segments are more detectable than the three irregular patterns (Patterns 1–3). However, there is no suggestion that any particular regularity of form is any more effective in increasing detectability than any other. All nine of the regular forms seem to be equivalently detectable.

The findings in both parts of this experiment point to a process of interaction between the parts that is quite different from the interaction of dots in a straight line. Indeed, one possible explanation concerning the effect observed in this experiment for the parallel lines (Patterns 7–12) is that an additional apparent line of dots is generated in each case. These additional lines are the ones produced by

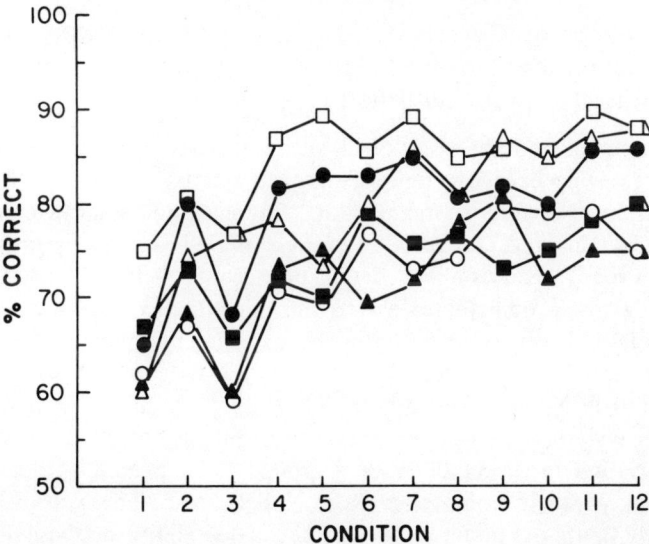

FIGURE 2-27 Graph showing the effect of the degree of organization of four line segments. With the exception of Stimulus 1 and 3, two of the pick-up-sticks patterns, all other patterns exhibited a relatively constant, higher level of detectability. Pattern 2 was also a pick-up-sticks pattern, but the experimenter inadvertently designed this pattern to have an axis of symmetry. That seems to be sufficient to raise the detectability to the levels of the other regular patterns. The results shown in this figure and in Fig. 2-26 suggest that any kind of order is sufficient to elevate detectability. Masking dot density: (□) 60; (●) 80; (△) 100; (■) 120; (○) 140; (▲) 160.

the vertical alignment of the horizontal bars, and vice versa. Therefore, there are in a certain sense more straight lines to be detected. However, because the effect seems to be independent, to a first approximation, of the spacing irregularity of these newly generated lines and because the scores with squares or triangles (Patterns 4–6) in each of the two groups of stimuli also display the enhancement to approximately the same degree, this is conclusive proof that this finding is not simply an extrapolation of the principle that lines are seen especially well. Instead, it must be concluded that some form of "organizational" interaction is occurring among the lines in a more subtle fashion.

C. Experiment X:
Even Further Effects of Figural Organization on Dotted-Form Detection

Having considered the effect of distorting squares into parallelograms and organizing lines into figures, the next related problem deals with another form of figural organization. Triangles and squares can also be considered to be composed of corners as well as sides, even though it has already been established that because of their reduced detectability, corners contribute less to the detectability of the polygons than sides. The question asked in this experiment concerns the interactions occurring between the corners of triangles and squares as measured in an experiment in which these parts are presented in a progressively less well-organized fashion. In this case, the concern is the variation in detectability of a group of component corners as a function of their coherence as a global form. The working hypothesis in this experiment is that the detectability of these figures should decrease as they are distorted into increasingly more irregular figures.

1. Stimuli. The stimulus patterns used in this experiment are shown in Figure 2-28. One set of patterns is composed of five-dot corners from triangles with the dots separated by 22.5' of visual angle. The patterns have been varied in such a way that an increasing, although arbitrary, amount of irregularity is introduced into the figure sequentially from the most regular pattern (Pattern 1) to the most irregular (Pattern 3). Pattern 4 is a single five-dot pattern equivalent to one of the corners. It was introduced into the experiment to provide a standard reference against which the interaction effects among three corners could be compared, as well as to demonstrate the reduced detectability of a single corner.

Figure 2-28 also displays patterns formed from the corners of squares. Patterns 1–4 are four-corner stimuli with a constant dot spacing maintained for all patterns. The corners, in this case, are composed of dots with a separation of 22.5' of visual angle. In Pattern 1, the four corners are arranged into a regular square but in Patterns 2–4 the forms have been sequentially degraded by displacing one or more of the corners. Pattern 5 is a single corner, again to be used

III. SOME EXPERIMENTS ON ORGANIZATION

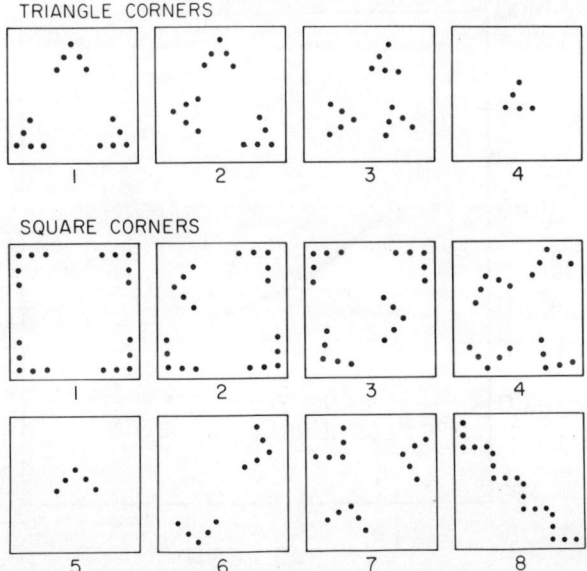

FIGURE 2-28 Sample target patterns used in the experiment determining the effect of polygonal pattern organization on detectability. In these figures, both triangles and squares have been disorganized by displacing one or more corners. Stimuli composed of one, two, or three corners or other regular patterns are also used.

as a reference standard, and Patterns 6 and 7 are two- and three-corner stimuli, respectively. Pattern 11 places the four corners in another regular order; in this case, however, it places the corners in a staircase arrangement rather than in a square, again to compare a highly ordered, but not square, stimulus with the square. A single noise density of 160 dots was chosen to demonstrate the effects of this form of pattern organization, after pilot studies showed this to be a suitable density capable of differentially masking all values of these highly detectable stimuli, yet minimizing "bottoming" and "topping" effects.

2. Results and discussion. The results for triangle corners are shown in Figure 2-29. As the degree of disorganization increases from Pattern 1 to Pattern 3, the detectability of the patterns correspondingly decreases, in spite of the fact that the stimulus patterns are all

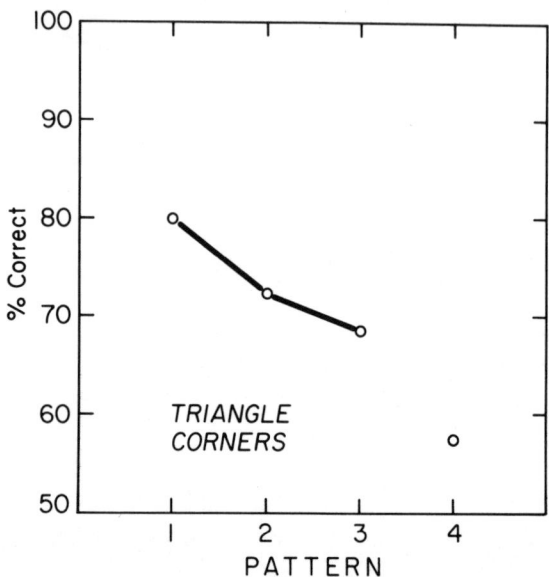

FIGURE 2-29 Graph showing the effect of pattern disorganization of triangles on their detectability. Increasing the disorder (patterns are as indicated in Fig. 2-28) reduces the detectability. A single corner is very difficult to see.

constant in terms of their component content and local interdot spacing. Pattern 4, the single corner, is substantially less detectable than even the most disorganized triangle; therefore, it must be assumed that there is some sort of residual interaction (possibly simple probability summation, but also possibly something more complex) reflected in the detection scores for the three-corner patterns, even when they are maximally disorganized.

The results of the experiment for the square corners are shown in Figure 2-30. Again, a progressive decline is seen in the detectability of the pattern as the four corners are increasingly perturbed from the most regular square configuration to the least regular configuration. Note also that any sort of order or arrangement seems capable of producing the necessary additional cues for enhanced detection, because there is little difference between the square pattern (Pattern 1) and the one (Pattern 8) in which the four corners are arranged

III. SOME EXPERIMENTS ON ORGANIZATION

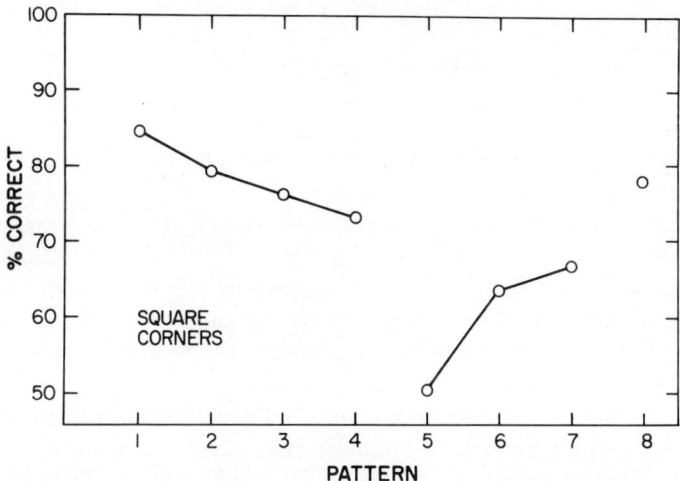

FIGURE 2-30 Graph showing the effect of pattern disorganization of squares on their detectability. Increasing the disorder (patterns are as indicated in Fig. 2-28) reduces their detectability. There is a progressive increase in detectability with increases in the number of corners; the staircase pattern is as easily seen as a regular square.

in staircase order. Furthermore, when only a single corner is presented, the score is substantially lower than that for even the most disorganized four-corner pattern, indicating that some sort of residual interaction among the corners, perhaps more profound than simple probability summation, is still occurring even under conditions of maximum disorganization. The nature and amount of this cumulative effect is further indicated by the comparison of the one-, two-, and three-corner stimuli (Patterns 5, 6, and 7) with the most disorganized square on the second curve of Figure 2-30. A progressive increase in the detectability of the stimuli is seen to occur as the number of corners increases.

The main thrust of these results is to further support the hypothesis that the global pattern or arrangement of a group of component parts is a strong determinant of pattern detectability. In this case, it is seen that increasing the "organization" of the pattern increases the psychophysical detectability.

D. Experiment XI:
The Effect of Ordered Figural Goodness on Dotted-Form Detection

The previous two experiments inquired into the effect of a relatively arbitrary and unscaled degree of organization and disorganization on the detectability of dotted patterns. They did not speak in a quantitative manner to the quality that the Gestalt psychologists referred to as "goodness" of form, however, because the stimuli were not metricized for goodness. For that matter, neither did the Gestaltists always quantify that dimension to the satisfaction of any of their successors. In recent years, goodness of form has again become an issue of considerable interest, and some investigators have been successful in defining the concept specifically enough that it can be used as a quantified independent variable.

For our purposes, by far the best quantification of goodness was carried out by Garner and Clement (1963), also using dot patterns. In one of their experiments, subjects were asked to rate the "goodness" of a series of arbitrary patterns constructed from a 3×3 dot matrix. The result of this procedure was a reliable ranking of the 17 patterns used and, satisfyingly, these rankings were also well-correlated inversely with the findings of a second experiment, in which subjects were asked to group the figures. Size of group and sorting time both declined as goodness increased. The present experiment investigates the effects of this kind of metricized figural goodness as a determinant of the detectability of dot patterns in dotted noise.

1. Stimuli. Garner and Clement's 17-dot patterns were used as stimuli, in a somewhat revised form. This 3×3 prototype dot matrix used by them was extended in this experiment to a 5×5 dot format to better coordinate with the other stimuli used in this study and to raise detectability levels to comparable levels. However, as much as possible of the original Garner and Clement configurations were maintained. The 17 patterns were presented in random order in varying amounts of dotted visual noise on sequential days. Both horizontal and vertical spacings in the 5×5 dot matrix were 39' of visual angle. This meant, it should be noted, that dotted lines that

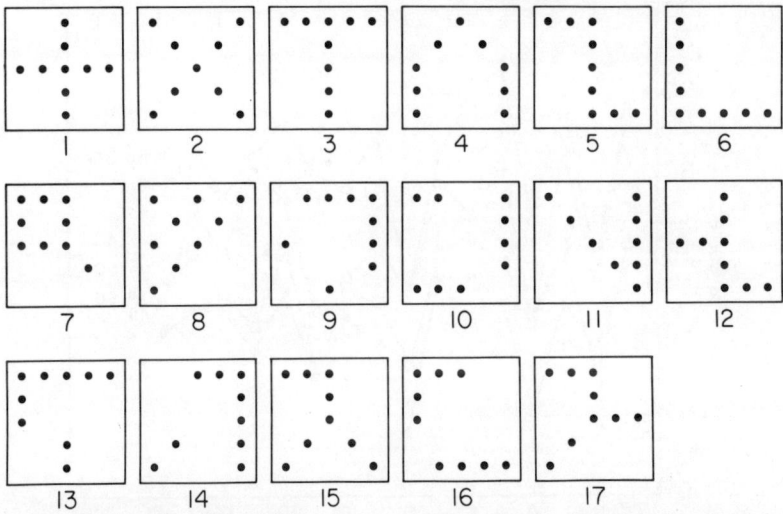

FIGURE 2-31 Sample target stimuli based on Garner and Clement's patterns used in the experiment determining the effect of figural "goodness" on detectability.

were aligned along diagonals actually had dot spacings of 55.1'. The specific stimulus patterns used are shown in Figure 2-31. Noise levels of 30, 40, 50, and 60 randomly placed dots were used to mask the various patterns, this being sufficient to scan the entire range of detectability performance with those stimuli.

2. Results and discussion. Results of this experiment have been plotted in Figure 2-32. For all levels of masking noise, it is clear that there is very little difference in the detection scores between figures that are classified by Garner and Clement as "good" and those that are not. The only noticeable difference is that scores for certain figures (2, 4, 8, and 11) are depressed below the recognition levels for the other characters. Inspection of these patterns indicates that major components are entirely, or in large part, oriented along diagonal lines. In these patterns, therefore, the dot spacing is in part greater than when the dotted lines are oriented vertically or horizontally, and the decrement in performance may be entirely attributed

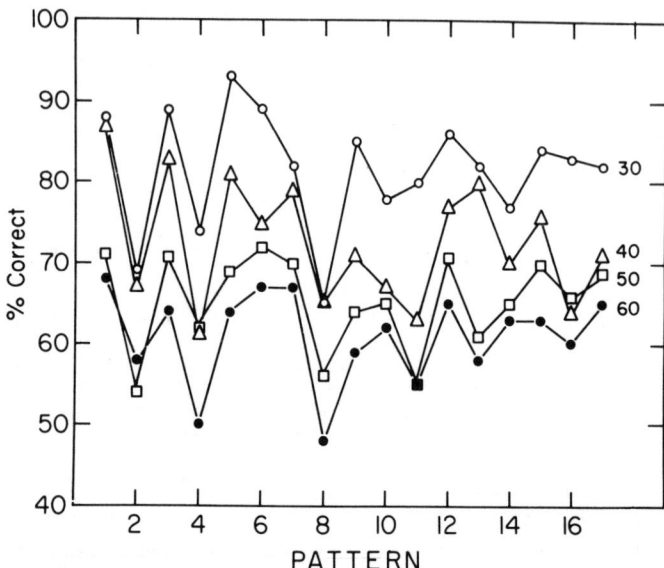

FIGURE 2-32 Graph showing the relatively minor effect of figural "goodness" on target detectability. Numbers in figure indicate the masking dot density: (○) 30; (△) 40; (□) 50; (●) 60.

to this factor. This effect of dot spacing is entirely consistent with the results of the previously reported experiments.

The major conclusion from this experiment is that the dimension scaled in Garner and Clement's experiment and designated as "figural goodness" is not a determinant of performance in the detection task required of the subjects in the present experiments. That the "goodness" Garner and Clement so reliably metricize is a determinant of other facets of human performance is beyond question. Discrimination, reaction times, and multidimensional information processing have all been shown to be so affected (Garner, 1974). Apparently, however, whatever the dimension of "goodness" may be, it operates in a somewhat different fashion when the subject is attempting to extract stimuli from noise in a detection task than when he is using the same stimuli as vehicles to convey multidimensional information to be used in the cognitive processing task assayed by the Garner and Clement experiment. In other words, "goodness" and "organization" are two quite different dimensions.

E. Experiment XII:
The Locus of the Dot-Masking Phenomenon

On the basis of the findings from earlier studies (Uttal, 1969, 1970) on dot masking that were carried out in the author's laboratory, the conviction had grown that the dot-masking effect was mainly a matter of confusion between the mixture of the dots of the mask and stimulus, caused by an overlap of persisting image traces. The paradigm thus seemed to be substantially explained by central information processing mechanisms that, although acting on the fused pattern to extract the signal from the noise, were more or less independent of the peripheral interactions characteristic of the Stage 2 processes. The idea of simple mixing because of persistence was a direct result of the early work that showed nearly symmetrical masking to be produced, respectively, by leading and trailing dynamic visual noise (see Figure 2-33). Further support for this notion was given by Schiller's (1966) work with a paradigm that involved the masking of letters by letters. His findings also displayed the presence of comparable

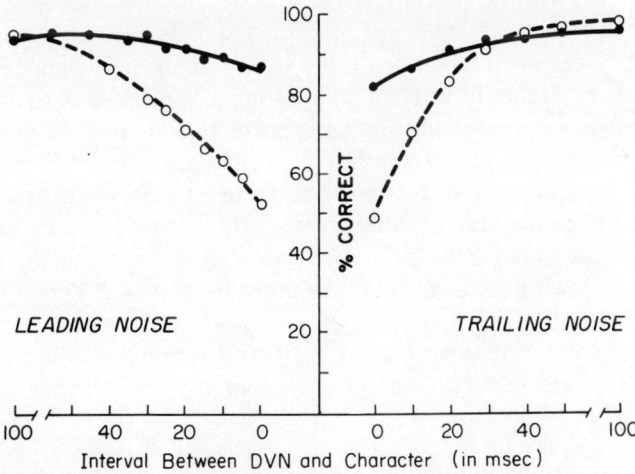

FIGURE 2-33 Graph showing the effect of leading and trailing noise, respectively, on the detectability of dotted alphabetic characters. "DVN" is temporally distributed noise. Noise dots were presented *ad seriatum* rather than in a simultaneous burst. (●) 3-msec DVN; (○) 1-msec DVN. (From Uttal, 1969.)

amounts of forward and backward masking. Both Uttal's and Schiller's experiments, however, used a binocular (i.e., same stimulus to both eyes) viewing procedure.

Support for a central locus of those masking effects was obtained in studies of dichoptic (i.e., different parts of the stimulus to each eye) metacontrast (Kolers & Rosner, 1960) and dichoptic backward masking (Schiller, 1965). Everything thus seemed to fit together to support a theory that invoked a central locus for dot-masking effects. Therefore, the conviction grew that producing a cluttered image in which a signal was hidden in a confusing array of dots involved nothing other than a simple merging of stimuli. A central mechanism that extracted the signal pattern from the noise pattern seemed sufficient to explain all of the results.

However, in a notable study, Turvey (1973) has shown that the one condition which, unfortunately, was not examined in any of the previous studies, dichoptic forward masking, produces very different results.* His findings are exceedingly important; in fact, almost all contemporary theories regarding the nature of the masking effect must be substantially altered if Turvey's conclusion is correct. In view of the very significant consequences that Turvey's findings conceivably could have for contemporary theory, it is especially important that they be substantiated for the dot-masking paradigm. Because a number of closely related, but distinguishable, types of masking are known, a considerable amount of care must be used before generalizing from one type to another. The general theme of Turvey's research is to distinguish between two kinds of masking depending on the nature of the masker. Similarly, it is important to make sure that a third type is not introduced in the present study; the main purpose of the following experiment is therefore to replicate Turvey's paradigm, but with dot patterns.

Specifically, the experiment sought to determine whether forward dichoptic masking was present or absent for this type of stimulus

---

* The following discussion of Turvey's finding concerns those aspects of his work that deal with the masking of letters by letter fragments—the situation that is comparable to the masking of dot patterns by dotted noise used in the present study. In those situations in which he uses a random noise mask to mask letters, the masking is apparently peripheral and actually more like masking by bright flashes than the dot noise masking of the present paradigm. In this latter case, the random field simply acts like a bright flash.

III. SOME EXPERIMENTS ON ORGANIZATION

material. To answer this question, two steps were required: first, monoptic, binocular, and dichoptic forward masking were compared; then, in a second part of the experiment, a comparison was made between dichoptic forward and backward masking to guarantee that the obtained diminution in forward dichoptic masking was not caused by some artifact of the dichoptic procedure. For reasons of scheduling, the two parts of the experiment were carried out on different groups of subjects; therefore, comparisons of the absolute levels of the results of the two parts of the experiment would not be meaningful.

1. Stimuli. The stimulus patterns were the same as those used in Experiment VII. Triangles and squares, rotated to a number of different orientations, were presented in specified amounts of dotted visual noise. In the first part of the experiment, stimuli were presented in one of three forward masking conditions. In the first condition, the subject viewed the oscilloscope display screen with both eyes and the noise dots and the pattern were physically superimposed. In the second condition, the subject viewed the same display but with only one eye, the other being blocked by an eyepatch. In the third condition, the stimuli were presented on either side of a split-screen display that operated as a stereoscope. The leading noise was presented randomly on one side of the screen or the other and the stimulus pattern on the opposite side, while the subject viewed the split screen (the two parts of which were separated by an opaque septum) through a pair of converging lenses adjusted for comfortable fusion. The image, therefore, was fused dichoptically into a single experience in which the stimulus and mask appeared to overlap.

This first part of the experiment showed virtually no masking in the forward dichoptic condition with 100 masking dots, but it did show strong masking for the forward monocular and binocular viewing conditions with the same number of masking dots. The second part of the experiment replicated the forward dichoptic masking condition and added to it a backward dichoptic masking condition as a comparison standard. In addition, the number of masking dots was increased to 200 to accentuate any differences between forward and backward masking conditions. The experimental design of the second part of the experiment, in which several variables were simultaneously varied, is shown in Figure 2-34.

2. THE PSYCHOPHYSICAL EXPERIMENTS

FORWARD MASKING

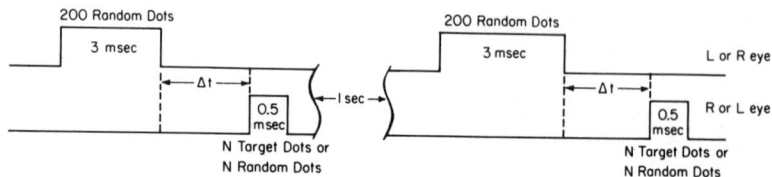

BACKWARD MASKING

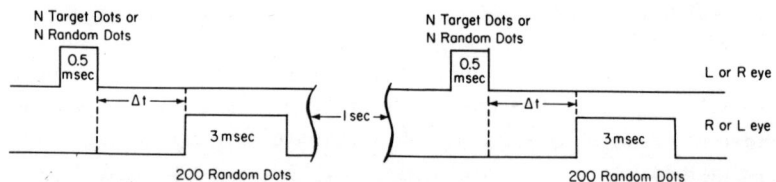

FIGURE 2-34 Diagrammatic presentation of the design of the experiment determining the locus of the dot masking effect.

Two possible artifacts had to be controlled in this experiment. One, which would have falsely argued against a peripheral locus for the masking effect, was a potential difficulty that might have led to an apparent masking under binocular viewing conditions when, indeed, there was none. Any error in the convergence or rotation of the eyes might have resulted in the stimulus and noise dots to each eye being fused centrally in such a way that would have led to a false "self-masking" merely because of the misregistration of the stimuli. In the monocular and binocular conditions of the first part of the experiment, therefore, no visual feedback and no fixation points of any kind were used. An auditory beep (low for incorrect, high for correct) was used as a feedback signal. In this manner, any discrepancy between monocular and binocular viewing conditions would have been accentuated because the subjects would have had no fixation cues other than the briefly flashed stimulus itself. The other possible artifact concerned the dichoptic conditions. If for any reason the subject did not properly converge, the stimulus dot pattern and the random noise dots would not be superimposed but would be seen side by side. In the dichoptic condition of the first part of the experiment and the two dichoptic conditions of the second part, therefore, a pair of fixation dots was presented to aid the subject in attaining optimal convergence. The pair of fixation dots, one of which was centrally located within each eye's field of view, was displayed between each stimulus presentation period of the trial cycle. The subjects were instructed not to respond until the two dots were fused, indicating proper convergence (the previous response to the stimulus released the next trial). Although it was possible for the subjects to deconverge intentionally, the great difference between the results of the forward and the backward dichoptic masking conditions and sample runs by the experimenter made it clear that this was not occurring.

Each of the five conditions was carried out separately. Within each condition, the interval between the mask and the stimulus pattern was decreased on successive days; the delays were sequentially set at values selected from among 60, 50, 40, 30, 20, 10, and 1 msec.

2. Results and discussion. The results of the three conditions of the first part of this experiment are shown in Figure 2-35. The results were clear-cut. Of the three forward masking conditions tested, monocular and binocular presentations led to a typical level and duration of forward masking. Dichoptic presentation of the same stimuli, however, produced virtually no masking. The results of the second part of the experiment are shown in Figure 2-36. Clearly, this comparison of forward and backward dichoptic conditions substantiated the finding that only the forward dichoptic masking condition was poor in masking efficacy. The backward masking condition again produced a typical response curve. The findings from the two parts of the experiment are summarized in Table 2-2.

These results speak to two separate issues. First, they are consistent with the conclusion that dot masking is a phenomena of the central nervous system, not of the periphery. The finding that there is strong dichoptic backward masking and weak dichoptic forward masking concurs with Turvey's data for similar conditions, in which letters were masked by letter fragments and in which simple stimulus energetics did not play a substantial role. Clearly, we might conclude, as he did for comparable conditions, that the processes assayed in

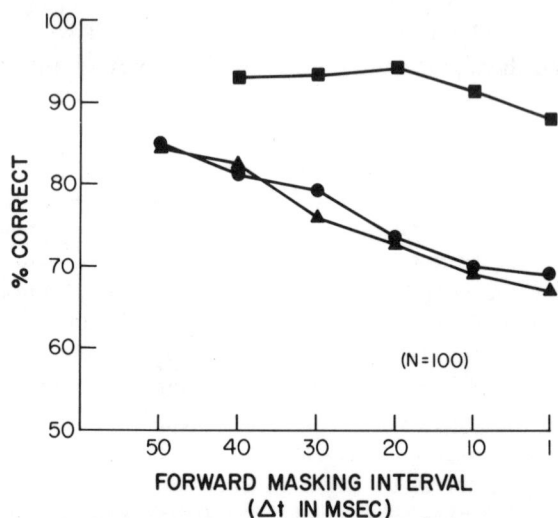

FIGURE 2-35 Graph showing the effects of three different viewing conditions on forward masking. Monocular (●) and binocular (▲) forward masking are nearly symmetrical with backward masking, but forward dichoptic masking (■) is very weak. Only 100 masking dots were used in this experiment.

the present study were those of a central, not a peripheral, information-processing mechanism.

Second, the present findings raise a serious question concerning the use of simple temporal overlap as a theoretical construct. Because of the asymmetry of the forward and backward dichoptic masking conditions, one is forced to reconsider any theory based on the simple persistence of a briefly stored "icon." However, even this simple notion may be partially salvaged by invoking a well-known fact about the recognition of forms; namely, it takes a finite amount of time to process the image. Sperling (1963), for example, has shown that the typical time for an unmasked alphabetic character to be recognized is about 10 msec, and that this processing time seems to increase linearly as more characters are added. For all intervals greater than some similar value between a leading mask and a trailing stimulus (forward masking), a sufficient difference between the residual brightness of the icon of the mask and of the target stimulus has developed, allowing processing of the stimulus. This is another way of saying, as Turvey (1973) did, that "when two stimuli compete for the services of a central decision processor, the victor is likely

III. SOME EXPERIMENTS ON ORGANIZATION

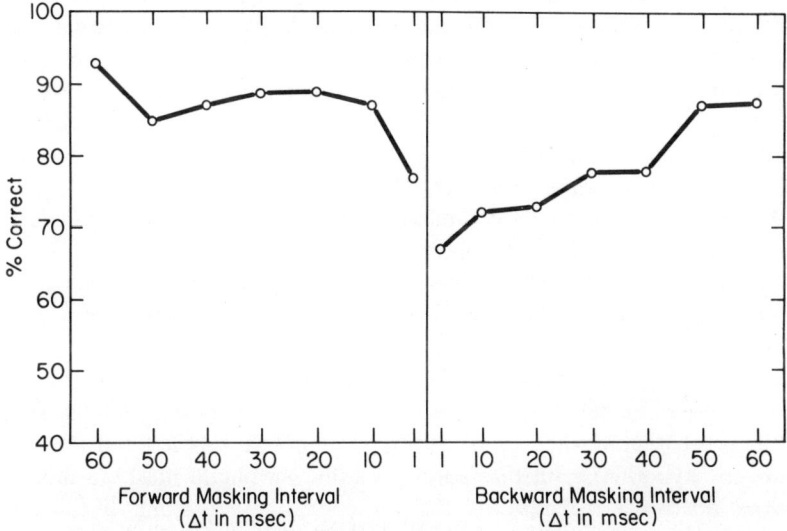

FIGURE 2-36 Graph comparing the effects of forward and backward dichoptic masking. Forward dichoptic masking is still very weak, even though the masking dot density has been increased to 200.

to be the one that arrives second [p. 39]." In other words, an "infinite" amount of time is really available to process the trailing stimulus as long as the interval between the leading mask and the trailing stimulus is greater than a minimum value. When the mask follows the stimulus, however, it interferes with the detection of the stimulus by cluttering up its icon before it can be fully processed. In the latter case, when the interval between stimulus and mask is short, stimulus processing is interfered with because of the effect of the trailing mask-

TABLE 2-2
Effectiveness of Masking in Six Different Masking Conditions

	Forward	Backward
Monocular	Yes	Yes
Binocular	Yes	Yes
Dichoptic	No	Yes

ing dots. Increases in the interval allow progressively greater amounts of processing time and therefore progressively higher detection scores.

In sum, the locus of the backward dot-masking procedure is clearly central and the initial notion that dot masking is caused by the overlap of the temporally dispersed traces of the fused images may still stand, qualified only by Sperling's notion of a finite processing time for individual forms. However, all of this is inconsistent with any theory that assumes that dot masking is mediated by any mechanism involving brightness inhibition of one set of dots by another.

What is left unexplained is why the effects of forward dichoptic masking, on the one hand, and forward monocular or binocular masking, on the other, should show such a difference in magnitude. Because of this dilemma, a general explanation of all dot masking based solely on a central model is not viable. Turvey's striking findings and the present confirmation of them precludes a simple "tail of the image" hypothesis. Furthermore, a totally peripheral masking model does not work because of the presence of the strong backward dichoptic masking effect. Therefore, what we are left with is a general explanation that, as Turvey has so eloquently spelled out, must be based on multiple mechanisms—not the most parsimonious explanation, but one necessitated by the data. This model states that there are both peripheral and central aspects to certain masking conditions.* Nevertheless, because all of the masking data on the effects of form in the present study have been collected using dots as both target stimuli and noise and a backward masking paradigm, the present set of experiments assays a process that, all agree, must be predominantly central.

Note added in proof: It has been pointed out by Professor Phipps Arabie of the University of Minnesota that there was, indeed, one early example of an experiment (M. Kinsbourne & E. K. Warrington, *The Quarterly Journal of Experimental Psychology,* 1962, **14,** 235–245.) in which dichoptic masking was tested and found to be present. If Kinsbourne and Warrington were correct and Turvey and Uttal were wrong, life would be much simpler.

---

* However, the reader must be very careful to note what Turvey specifically means by "peripheral" and "central." His peripheral mechanisms include part of the visual cortex.

3
The Theory

I. A SUMMARY OF THE EXPERIMENTAL FINDINGS

The results of the experiments carried out in this study, along with some other relevant data, present a fairly complete description of a moderately restricted form of visual perception—the type of processing that we refer to as a "Stage 3" function. The features of dotted lines and polygons that are important in defining their detectability in dotted visual noise are therefore now beginning to be identified. It is useful at this point to summarize the experimental findings preparatory to presenting the theoretical model. Each summary statement is, of course, framed within a context in which all other variables are held constant. No assertion is made about the relative magnitudes of the various effects or about which effect is dominant in a situation in which two or more dimensions are concomitantly varying.

The following list summarizes what we now believe to be the basic findings concerning Stage 3 processing obtained with the dotted signal–noise paradigm:

1. The detectability of a straight dotted line strongly depends on the distance between the constituent dots, even when the dot spacing greatly exceeds the acuity threshold.

2. The detectability of a straight dotted line depends on the number of dots in a straight line up to limits imposed by the span of the subject's visual field and, possibly, also on some lesser limiting distance for the interaction between dots.

3. The detectability of a straight dotted line in dotted noise is insensitive to the orientation of that line.

4. The detectability of a straight dotted line is superior to that of a curved or angled line, and the decline in detectability is monotonic with increases in curvature or angulature.

5. The detectability of dotted straight lines with irregular spacings (but with collinearity maintained) is substantially less than that of a regularly spaced straight line. This finding implies that dot spacing regularity (i.e., spatial periodicity) is highly significant in defining the detectability of a pattern.

6. Deviations from collinearity also exert strong disruptive effects on the detectability of a straight line.

7. The sides of dotted triangles are considerably more decisive for their recognizability than the corners, despite the higher information content of the less redundant dots of the corners. Indeed, deleting dots that describe corners has no greater effect on detectability than removing an equal number of randomly selected dots. This effect may be a simple reflection of the fact that dotted lines are more easily seen than corners in visual noise.

8. The detectabilities of dotted triangles and squares, the prototypical polygons, are insensitive to their orientations.

9. Distortion of a regular dotted pattern (a square) into a less regular pattern (a parallelogram) leads to a monotonic decline in its detectability.

I. A SUMMARY OF THE EXPERIMENTAL FINDINGS 91

10. Organization of a set of dotted lines into regular polygonal forms or linear arrays enhances detectability over that of irregular arrangements. As a first approximation, this result appears to be independent of the nature of the regular form. A set of four parallel lines is equally as detectable as a square, even when the parallel lines are not evenly spaced. This suggests the presence of an additional form of interaction: lines or corners can interact with each other just as the dots that compose the line or corner interact with each other.

11. Disorganization of the component corners of squares and triangles from regular arrangements into increasingly less regular arrangements decreases the detectability of the form in a monotonic fashion.

12. "Figural goodness," as defined by Garner and Clement, has little effect on the detectability of figures. Most deviations in detectability can be accounted for in terms of such basic parameters as dot density. Apparently, this form of figural goodness is not identical to the variation of component parts in the experiments on organization.

13. A comparison of forward and backward masking effects presented under dichoptic conditions demonstrates that the backward dot-masking effects under consideration in this study are mediated, in major part, by the central nervous system. At the same time, this study confirms Turvey's (1973) finding that forward dichoptic masking is much less effective than backward dichoptic masking for equivalent delays and noise densities and that forward monocular masking is strong. Although this remains a perplexing inconsistency, the weight of the evidence is that the backward dot-masking phenomena of the present study on form detection are mediated by a central process.

It should be noted that a number of other general features of human form recognition are well accepted and must also be included in any formal model that lays claim to more than the most limited generality. For example, it is clear that form recognition, in general, is not strongly influenced by translation or magnification. The size of the pattern and where it is placed in the visual field exert only secondary effects on recognition or detection accuracy. Indeed, even the viewing angle plays a remarkably minor role. It is also clear that any explanation of form detection must include an explanation of how an observer can recognize objects that he has never seen before or has never seen before in a particular orientation. Similarly, how is it that a caricature or a silhouette, as well as a dot pattern (all representative classes of stimuli that present only partial cues), can be processed in a manner that leads to recognition almost as readily as the most highly pictographic mappings are processed and recognized?

These sorts of first-approximation considerations suggest that any theory based on stored templates or standards against which incoming information must be compared (as is required by a cross-correlation theory) will have a difficult time explaining many aspects of human form recognition. Furthermore, any such theory that postulates stored templates, rather than rules of algorithmic processing, immediately encounters simple numerical difficulties in terms of adequate storage space and exhaustive search times required to make the necessary comparisons between the input stimuli and the postulated set of templates. Arguments of information economy therefore support an algorithmic approach.

It is far more compelling to invoke a mechanism that operates on stimuli in such a way that the recognition criteria are carried along with the stimulus itself. An important point implicit in the preceding statement that must be stressed repeatedly concerns the key premise of each theory with regard to where the recognition criteria are to be localized. Any physiologically oriented single-cell or multicell theory, which assumes that the neurons of the brain are feature filters that display some special sensitivity to one or another feature of the stimulus, localizes the decision criteria in the neurons themselves. Quite the contrary, an algorithmic theory, which assumes that a relatively small set of very general transforms are applied to the stimuli, is based on the very different premise that there is a primitive, but fundamental, quality of the stimulus itself that determines its recognizability. Therefore, such algorithmic theories must be based on the premise that the recognition criteria are intrinsic to the stimuli and that, perhaps, several different transforms may have the ability to extract the same critical information.

This is not to say that the stimuli may be perceived without an observer or that the information processing mechanism of the observer plays no contributory role. Rather, this approach emphasizes that, when all other factors are held constant, there are still certain aspects of the stimulus that define and delimit their detectability. For a given observer, some patterns are more detectable than others. Identifying those defining aspects of the stimulus is the problem at hand.

The point cannot be overemphasized that the particular theory to be presented in the next section is probably only one of a number of nearly equivalent, transformationally oriented approaches. The essence of this particular approach lies largely in its emphasis on the externalization of the recognition criteria in the stimulus, rather than in the neurons of the nervous system.

Is there a model that not only displays the general characteristics of human form perception but also displays the specific response characteristics of the psychophysical results obtained in this study? A highly likely candidate is the autocorrelation transform used previously by Dodwell (1971) and Engel (1969) among others and described in Chapter 1, Section III.D.6. Autocorrelation mechanisms fit the general needs required of such a theory in surprisingly many ways. In the following sections, one form of such an autocorrelation model is considered and tested.

II. BASIC PROPERTIES OF THE AUTOCORRELATION MODEL

The notion that some sort of an autocorrelation model might be descriptive of many aspects of Stage 3 visual perception has been gaining wide acceptance in recent years. The specific suggestion that some kind of a neural mechanism, describable in the mathematical language of correlation, might be operating in the dot pattern detection paradigm with which our laboratory had been working was probably made first by Dodwell (1971). It also emerged in conversations among the author and his colleagues, James O. Chinnis, Jr., Joseph Mesrich, and Larry Goble, at The University of Michigan on the independent basis of what is believed to be the highly compelling force of our experimental findings.

3. THE THEORY

The basic notion of an autocorrelation theory of dotted pattern detection—the restricted universe of form recognition to which the present discussion is largely confined—is that a signal or target pattern is in some way extracted from the combined signal and noise stimulus on the basis of certain organizational characteristics of the stimulus array that the noise dots themselves do not possess. Autocorrelation mechanisms have the property of being able to extract regular or organized signals from quasi-random noise without reference to any criteria other than those contained in the signal itself. Indeed, the autocorrelation process requires only a single presentation of the pattern, unlike the averaging procedure, a related transform that can accomplish similar feats only on the basis of multiple exposures. It is also unlike the cross-correlation approach, which requires reference standards against which to compare the signal.

Simple one-dimensional autocorrelations accomplish signal extraction by making multiple representations or replicas of the input pattern by means of simple time delays or space shifts. The set of replicas is then compared (by multiplication or addition, then integration) to the original patterns. In this manner, periodic properties of the original pattern are enhanced or extracted when the time or space shifts are equal to the periods of the repetitive components of the pattern. The two-dimensional autocorrelation, necessary in the case of all but the most trivial of visual stimulus arrays, operates exactly in the same manner, except that the two-dimensional replicas are produced simply by shifting the original stimulus array by Δx and Δy in an x, y space. Cross products of the shifted and the original stimulus are then computed for each point in the shifted space and a new matrix in the $\Delta x, \Delta y$ space is accordingly defined, following a two-dimensional or double integration [see Eq. (1-1)].

Therefore, the basic result of this shift, compare, and integrate operation is to produce another function in the $\Delta x, \Delta y$ space that is a transform of the original stimulus in the x, y space. In this transform, the periodic, repetitive, or some otherwise organized aspects of the original patterns are enhanced to a greater degree than the periodic or disorganized features in the transform space.

The transformed array may look very little like the original pattern because high cross products can occur where there has been nothing

II. BASIC PROPERTIES OF THE AUTOCORRELATION MODEL 95

in the original pattern, and vice versa. Furthermore, there are always more elements to the autocorrelated transform than there are to the original stimulus pattern. Amplitude differences between the components in the transform are also created, even where all components of the original stimulus may have been of equal intensity.

The autocorrelation function, like the psychophysical data, displays a particularly high sensitivity to the periodic properties of the stimulus. It is this feature, along with the fact that no secondary template or standard is required for pattern extraction (the latter being, admittedly, a criterion of parsimony and "elegance" rather than a compelling quantitative proof), that has provided the major initial impetus for the selection of this particular transform as the theoretical model.

Another general characteristic of the autocorrelation transform, and a good clue to whether or not a true autocorrelation transform* is being generated with some analog or digital computation device, is that the cross product must be at a maximum when Δx and Δy are both zero. Therefore, any autocorrelation must display a bright central spot at the 0, 0 point in the $\Delta x, \Delta y$ space. The amplitude of this central spot is solely a function of the number and amplitude of the dots in the original stimulus pattern but, unlike the other parts of the autocorrelogram, it is independent of their form or arrangement.

In summary, a parallel processing, autocorrelating model of visual form detection is here proposed of the following form:

$$A_c = \int \int f(x,y) \cdot f(x + \Delta x, y + \Delta y) \, dy \, dx. \qquad (3\text{-}1)$$

An important basic notion concerning autocorrelation is that the implementation of the transform is based on shifting and multiplying operations that do not involve specialized (that is, feature-specific or feature-sensitive) constituent neural elements. In fact, parallel organized homogeneous sheets of materials, such as photographic film, make excellent autocorrelators; indeed, the first device used in our laboratory to autocorrelate dotted stimulus patterns was a simple,

---

* In fact, an early version of the optical autocorrelator to be described shortly produced a misleadingly similar but incorrect transform.

shoebox-like optical analog computer (McLachlan, 1962; Meyer-Eppler, 1946; Meyer-Eppler & Darius, 1956; Philips & McLachlan, 1954).

There is no a priori need, then, to require any special directional properties, such as the Hubel and Wiesel cortical feature-sensitive neurons exhibit, or to postulate any specialized neurons that possess Fourier-like spatial frequency specificity. The only requirement is the presence of some kind of neural mechanism that can provide analogs of the shifting operations, of either an additive or multiplicative sort of cross-product generator, and of an integrator or summator.

The major remaining question, after matters of preference and first approximation are resolved, is: Does the transform correspond closely enough to the psychophysical data to be acceptable as a model of the visual process? In the following sections, our goal is to first explain the details of a computer simulation of the autocorrelation model and then to use the simulation to carry out comparisons of the computer simulations and the psychophysical data to answer this question. Some speculative physiological mechanisms that may embody details of the model are then projected.

III. A COMPUTER SIMULATION OF THE AUTOCORRELATION MODEL

A computer program embodying the autocorrelation transform, presented in Eq. (1-1), was developed to explore the applicability of the model to dotted-form detection. The simulation model is designed to allow on-line operation with a rapid display of the transformed matrices onto either of two output media: a line printer for specific numerical values or an oscilloscope for graphic representation. Stimulus patterns are entered into the system as arrays of 0 and 1 through the paper tape recoder under control of an acquisition subroutine: 0 indicates the absence of a stimulus dot; 1 indicates the presence of a stimulus dot. The matrix size used for the introduction of the stimulus patterns was variable up to a maximum of 63×63. Of course, as the matrix size increased, the processing time required for the calculation of the autocorrelation transform also rapidly increased. All of the autocorrelations to be presented were done on either a 15×15 or a 20×20 input matrix.

III. A COMPUTER SIMULATION OF THE AUTOCORRELATION MODEL

As an expedient to reduce the computer processing time required for each autocorrelation (the calculations were carried out on the same small, 12-bit laboratory control computer used to run the psychophysical experiments), a simpler approximating algorithm was used. Instead of actually carrying out the multiplications or integrations, the integral was computed in the following manner for each $\Delta x, \Delta y$.

Assume that a stimulus pattern such as that indicated by the symbols 1 and 0 in Figure 3-1 is to be autocorrelated. This figure also portrays a replica of the pattern that is produced by shifts of $\Delta x = -3$ and $\Delta y = +3$ with the symbols 1' and 0'. The rules for simulating the autocorrelation are as follows:

1. If a position in the overlapping fields of the shifted and unshifted patterns contains both a 1' and a 1, add 16 to the value of the autocorrelation integral.

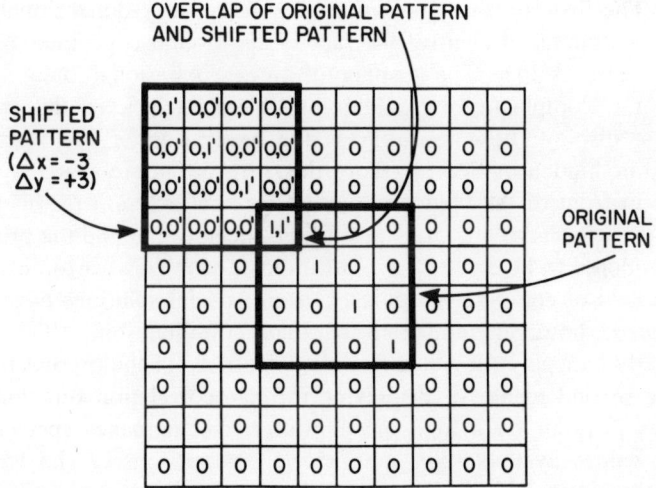

FIGURE 3-1 Diagram illustrating the procedure by which the autocorrelation was computed with the model. An original stimulus pattern was shifted to a new position (in this case by $\Delta x = -3$ and $\Delta y = 3$). The product of each overlapping block in the space was then computed as described in the text. Each block in this space should have two numbers in it, but to avoid cluttering this figure the two values have only been shown for the area of the shifted pattern. After shifting to a given Δx and Δy, the sum of the products is computed, thus simulating the double integration.

2. If a position contains a 1 or a 1' and a 0, add 4 to the value of the autocorrelation integral.
3. If a position contains only zeros, add 1 to the value of the autocorrelation integral.

The algorithm thus accumulates (simulating the process of integration) the set of numbers so generated for each position into a single autocorrelation value C_a for each Δx, Δy shift. The full set of autocorrelated values for all Δx, Δy shifts thus defines a new matrix—the autocorrelation function (C_a)—in the Δx, Δy space.

To achieve a better graphic quality, the computer program contains an algorithm designed to normalize this matrix by subtracting a number equal to the smallest value obtained from all values to form the final matrix. This normalization removes what would appear as a uniform pedestal in the graphic display and reduces the absolute magnitude of all values by a constant amount.

As noted, this output matrix may be displayed in either of two ways. The first is an isometric diagram of the three-dimensional (Δx, Δy, C_a) function drawn on the face of the oscilloscope (see, for example, Fig. 3-26). The display of three-dimensional data in this manner is complicated by a major problem intrinsic to this sort of graphic display: how to suppress the generation of the lines that should be hidden by those parts of the surface that are spatially interposed in front of the "hidden" part. A general solution to this problem for all forms of line drawings has not been found and the problem is considered to be one of the most difficult problems yet to be solved in the field of computer graphics. Certain special solutions have been produced, however, and one of them (Williamson, 1972) was adapted to display the autocorrelation matrices in the present model.

The second means of displaying the autocorrelation function is a tabular printout on a high-speed printer, which makes specific numeric values available for quantitative comparisons of the features of the various autocorrelograms.

IV. THEORY OF THE MODEL

As will be seen, the autocorrelograms produced by the model are, in general, more complex patterns than the original stimuli. The task of making comparisons between the various autocorrelograms is

IV. THEORY OF THE MODEL

therefore a more complex pattern recognition task than that asked of the subject when he is presented with the original stimuli. The next part of the problem thus becomes one of finding simple criterion indices or figures of merit that are able to summarize by a single number the results of the autocorrelation transform of each stimulus pattern. We must ask if there is some simple figure of merit representative of the features of the autocorrelograms that correlates with the psychophysical measures of detectability of the corresponding stimulus patterns.

It is proposed here that an affirmative answer to this question can be derived from the fact that the autocorrelation function transforms the important spatial features of the stimuli into an array in which amplitude and distance characteristics become decisive. Specifically, it is hypothesized that interaction among the amplitude and distance parameters of the peaks in the transform space define the detectability of the patterns.

In a first attempt to formulate a figure of merit for the individual autocorrelations, a simple measure of the maximum height of a peak or a row of peaks was used. However, it became clear immediately that an additional factor reflecting some kind of an interaction between peaks was also necessary; maximum peak height alone did not adequately predict the psychophysical findings. Examination of the autocorrelograms indicated that individual peaks must have been interacting with other peaks in some manner.

What clues are there, then, to the specification of an expression for the figure of merit that would include such interactions between peaks? Because the geometrical organization of the original stimulus patterns leads both to variations in the height of the peaks and to variations in the detectability of the stimulus, some algebraic interaction between the amplitudes of the autocorrelogram peaks seems necessary. Because decreased spacing between stimulus dots enhances detectability, and because this stimulus spacing is also reflected in spacing between peaks in the autocorrelogram, the figure of merit must also involve a distance function. On the basis of an examination of some of the autocorrelograms, it also seems likely that the absolute number of peaks in the autocorrelogram should also influence the figure of merit if it is to have any predictive capability. Specifically, when equated for energy content (i.e., the same number of stimulus dots and the same local geometry of interdot spacing), those stimulus patterns that contained fewer peaks seemed to be the most easily detected.

On the basis of such strictly empirical considerations as these and several attempts with alternative formulations, an arbitrary expression of the following form is suggested for the figure of merit.

$$F = \frac{\sum_{n=1}^{N} \sum_{i=1}^{N} (A_n \times A_i)/d_{ni}}{N} \qquad (n \neq i), \qquad (3\text{-}2)$$

where A_n = amplitude of nth peak; A_i = amplitude of ith peak; d_{ni} is the Pythagorean distance from the nth to the ith peaks in the Δx, Δy space, i.e., $[(\Delta x_n - \Delta x_i)^2 + (\Delta y_n - \Delta y_i)^2]^{1/2}$; and N = the total number of peaks.

The main axiom of the autocorrelation theory to be presented is that the interactions among the peaks of the autocorrelogram, as metricized by this algebraic expression for the figure of merit, are the key correlates of the psychophysical detectability of dotted stimulus patterns in dotted noise.

It must be kept clearly in mind why there are two steps—the autocorrelation transform and the calculation of the figure of merit—to this process. The autocorrelation is required because it is sensitive to the geometry, organizational pattern, or information content of the original stimulus. Carrying out the autocorrelation results in a pattern reflecting these properties in a way that the original pattern did not. Amplitude and spacing differences among the peaks are substituted for the unquantified pattern dimensions of the original stimulus. Autocorrelation, however, produces a pattern that is very complicated; some simple figure of merit must therefore be calculated in order to provide a metric suitable for the comparison of the various patterns. In the parallel processing environment of the brain, this latter operation may be unnecessary. One global state of the manifold of neural elements may be compared directly against another. When the computer model is applied, however, some figure of merit is required to enable the experimenter to make these comparisons.

To anticipate our findings, it will be shown that the more regular the stimulus pattern, the higher the figure of merit. It will be shown

IV. THEORY OF THE MODEL

further that the order of the figures of merit predicts the detectability scores obtained in the psychophysical experiments with very few exceptions.

First, however, let us consider, in the light of this interpretation, the general nature of the task of extracting signal dot patterns from random noise dots. How are observers able to see an ordered stimulus in what is often a much more dense pattern of visual noise dots?

To answer this question, examine the effects of autocorrelation on a simple stimulus pattern—the straight line composed of eight moderately spaced dots as shown in Figure 3-2a.

The autocorrelation transform of this line of dots is shown below it. This transform, a function in the $\Delta x, \Delta y$ space, is also in the form of a straight line. (As will be apparent, the congruence of the stimulus shape and the transform in this particular case is only fortuitous; transform shapes that differ greatly from the original stimulus are more usual.) This simple exemplar displays a number of the general features of the transform. Note that the amplitudes of the peaks corresponding to the stimulus dots decrease with increases in distance from the center of the $\Delta x, \Delta y$ space of the autocorrelogram. Furthermore, in accord with the general notion that the transforms are always more complex than the original stimuli, there are 15 peaks in the $\Delta x, \Delta y$ space, whereas there were only eight in the x, y space.

Now let us embed a similar eight-dot line stimulus pattern in random dotted noise. Such a stimulus, analogous to a single experimental trial of the present study, is shown in Figure 3-2b. Here, 13 randomly placed visual noise dots have been added to the target. The photograph shows the autocorrelated transform of this stimulus pattern. Note that the central peak is now considerably higher than in the transform of Figure 3-2a, reflecting the greater total number of dots and consequently a greater total stimulus energy.

Moreover, the peaks of the autocorrelogram that mainly correspond to the row of nine signal dots in this autocorrelation are larger in amplitude than the peaks that mainly correspond to the randomly placed noise dots. This is the key to the extraction of the pattern from the noise. The autocorrelation transform thereby has the effect of enhancing the amplitudes of the transforms of the periodic (organized) stimulus dots relative to the transforms of the randomly placed

102   3. THE THEORY

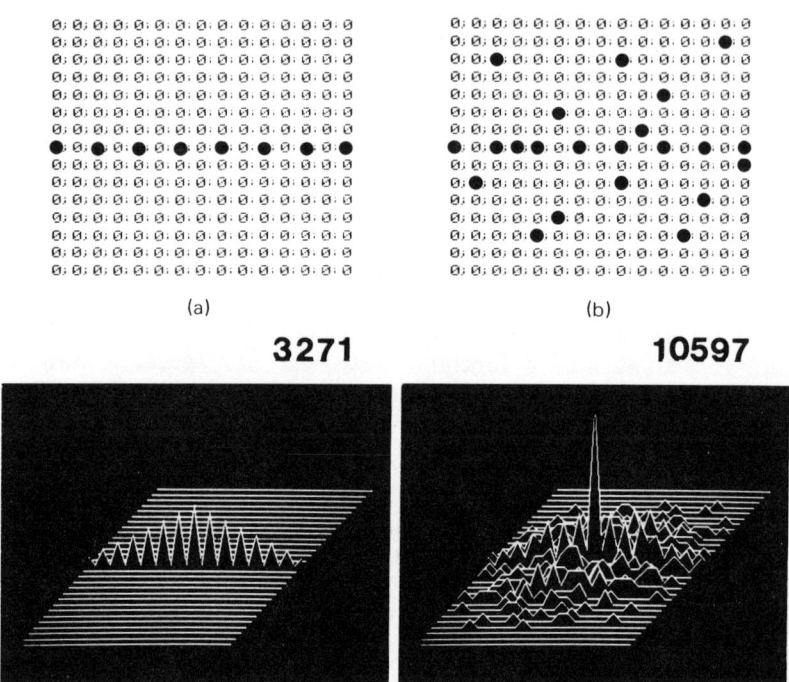

FIGURE 3-2 Sample autocorrelation plots showing (a) the autocorrelation of an eight-dot straight line, and (b) the autocorrelation of an eight-dot straight line mixed with 14 masking dots. Each autocorrelation plot is composed of three items: the simulated stimulus pattern, the graphic display of the autocorrelation space, and a number. The number is a figure of merit calculated as described in the text. Note that in (b) the peaks that are mainly the result of autocorrelating the straight line of dots are higher than the peaks that are mainly the result of random noise. This suggests a means based on the amplitude discrimination of autocorrelogram peaks by which regular patterns can be extracted from noisy backgrounds.

(disorganized) noise dots. On this basis, the autocorrelation transform, operating purely on the organizational properties of the stimulus, has converted a spatial arrangement of equal intensity dots in the x, y space into a group of dots with different intensities in the $\Delta x, \Delta y$ space.

This analysis specifically implies that the form discrimination task, originally presented to the subject as an equal energy dotted pattern, has been reencoded in the neural representation into a pattern with intensity differences between the peaks mainly associated with the regularly positioned stimulus dots and the peaks mainly associated with the irregularly positioned noise dots. This kind of dimensional change (in this case, from space to amplitude) is quite common within the nervous system and also well known in the auditory system. In the cochlea, time fluctuations in pneumatic pressure are converted into a neural representation using spatial localizations as a code. A complete discussion of dimensional changes in other sensory modalities can be found in Uttal (1973a).

The suggestion that the spatial pattern in the stimulus space has been reencoded into intensity differences in the autocorrelation space should not be interpreted to imply that the subjects must necessarily perceive these differences as brightness changes. The experimental paradigm used in this study does not directly clarify this issue; it is possible that subjects do perceive brightness differences, because they often report that stimuli "stand out" in a way that can be so interpreted. However, it is also possible that the autocorrelogram, varying as it does along a neural intensity dimension, is not perceived to be varying also in brightness. Instead, it may be seen exactly as the subject reports it—"I saw the pattern in the noise." In other words, there is no necessity for demanding isomorphism between the dimensions of the neural code and the perceived experience. (See Uttal, 1973a, for a further discussion of this point.)

V. TESTS OF THE MODEL

We now test the notion that the autocorrelation function is a good predictor of the effects of changes in the various stimulus dimensions examined in the experimental tests. In this section, an atlas of autocorrelograms is compiled and their respective figures of merit are calculated. The autocorrelograms are produced from a collection of patterns that correspond as closely as possible to the stimuli used in the psychophysical experiments. However, because of the coarseness of the grid used in the specification of the simulated stimuli for the autocorrelations (either a 15×15 or a 20×20 grid was used), slight deviations from the original stimulus patterns have been required in some instances. Specifically, with some of the patterns, reorienting a straight line from a horizontal to an oblique axis unavoidably increased the separation between the simulated stimulus dots. Therefore, the distance between the respective peaks in the autocorrelogram might have been increased artificially in a way that spuriously varied the figure of merit. In most cases in which this might have been a factor, it appeared that the artifact only modestly changed the magnitude, not the order, of the involved figures of merit.

Furthermore, to clarify the displays, only autocorrelograms of the simulated stimuli were presented. No noise dots were introduced, because only the relative effects of variations of a single stimulus dimension were of interest in each case. This procedure is acceptable because the transform of a constant number of random noise dots remains more or less constant from trial to trial and so can be ignored.

First, let us consider the effect of the number of dots in a straight line on the figures of merit of their respective autocorrelograms. The stimuli, the autocorrelograms, and the figures of merit are shown in Figure 3-3. Three stimuli with equal interdot spacing, each consisting of a single line with four, six, and eight dots, respectively, have been autocorrelated in this first example. Dot numerosity clearly has a strong effect on the amplitudes of the individual peaks of the autocorrelogram, with peak height increasing as the number of dots increases. This is reflected in the respective figures of merit for each autocorrelogram; values monotonically decrease with a decrease in the number of dots. The decrease in the figure of merit with decreased numerosity is in accord with the data obtained in the corresponding psychophysical experiment, where it has been shown that decreasing numerosity is associated with decreased detectability.

The effect of interdot spacing in a straight line of regularly spaced dots is examined next. The results are shown in Figure 3-4 for two stimulus conditions. Two lines, each containing five dots—one with one grid space between adjacent dots and one with two grid spaces between adjacent dots—have been autocorrelated. Again, the order of the figure of merit is in agreement with the psychophysical data. Increasing dot spacing produces a corresponding reduction in the

(a) **3271**

(b) **1513**

(c) **465**

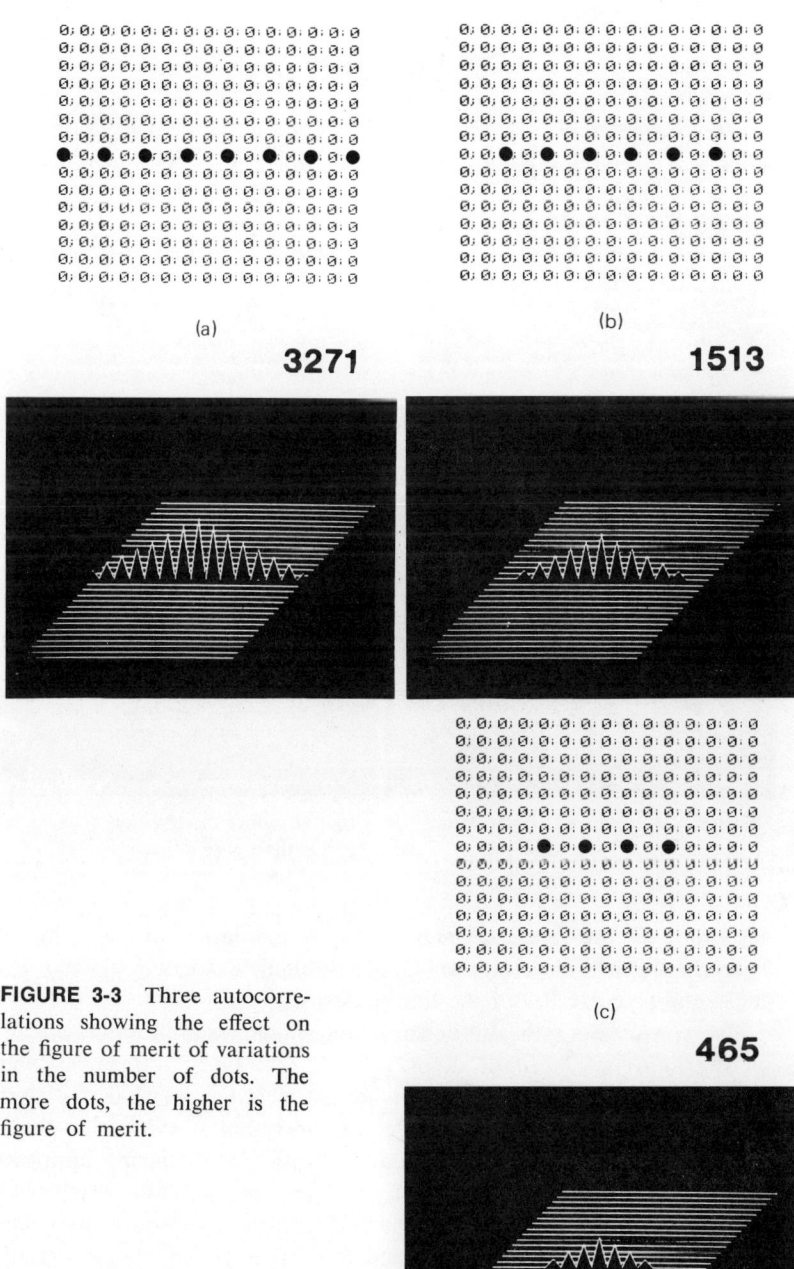

FIGURE 3-3 Three autocorrelations showing the effect on the figure of merit of variations in the number of dots. The more dots, the higher is the figure of merit.

3. THE THEORY

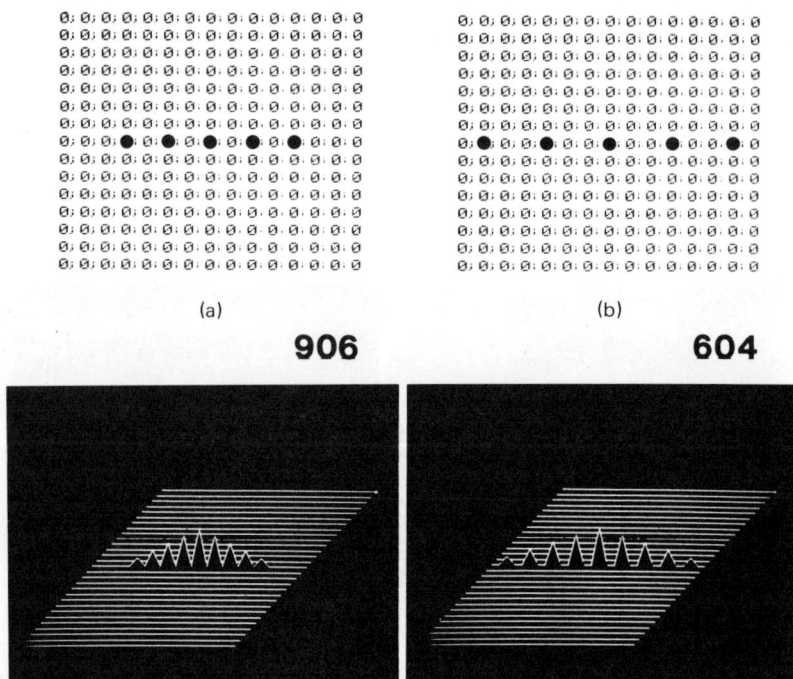

FIGURE 3-4 Two autocorrelations showing the effect on the figure of merit of dot spacing. The closer the dots, the higher is the figure of merit.

amplitude of the figure of merit, just as increasing dot spacing in a psychophysical experiment (Uttal, Bunnell, & Corwin, 1970) reduced the detectability of the line patterns.

The next test of the autocorrelation model examines the effects on the figure of merit of deforming straight lines into angles and curves. Figure 3-5 consists of four autocorrelations. The first is that of a seven-dot straight line; the second consists of a seven-dot pattern that has been deformed into a curve (with equal spacing approximated as closely as the coarse 15×15 matrix allowed to that of the straight line). The third and fourth are seven-dot patterns in which the straight line has been deformed into an angle of approximately 135° and 110°, respectively. The autocorrelograms of these four patterns are particularly interesting because they show, for the first time

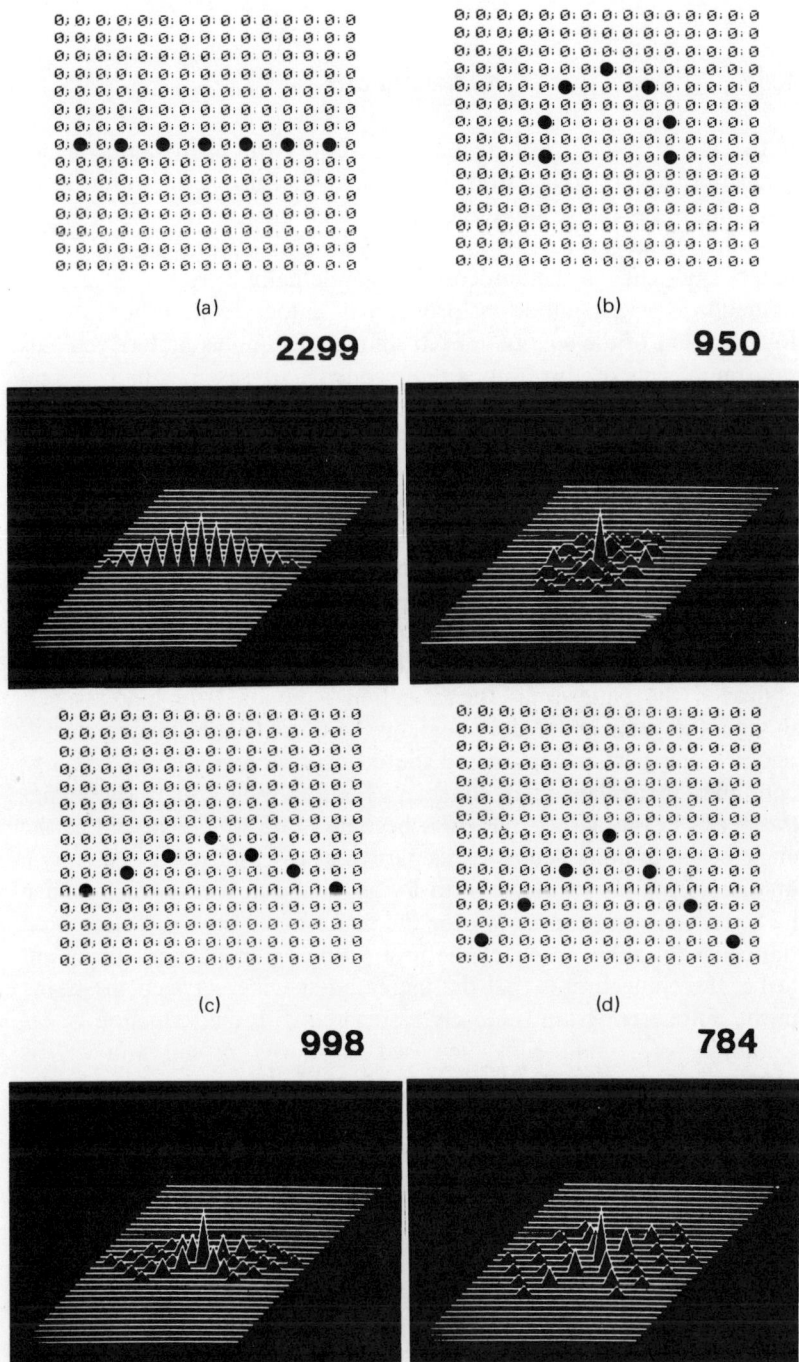

FIGURE 3-5 Four autocorrelations showing the effect of angulature and curvature on the figure of merit. The greater the deviation from linearity, the lower is the figure of merit (but see footnote on page 108).

in this series of tests, a change in the overall form of the autocorrelogram that results solely from changes in the global organization of the pattern. As the straight line is deformed into a curve or an angle, the autocorrelogram changes from a line into patterns in which the number of peaks in the autocorrelogram actually increases. This phenomenon is a very important property of autocorrelation because the total amount of the energy in each simulated stimulus pattern remains constant; each of the four stimuli consists of seven equally bright dots. Therefore, the amount of energy that can be allocated to each peak in the autocorrelogram must, on the average, decrease if the number of peaks increases. Energy distribution in the autocorrelogram is, therefore, very much a function of the global organization of the original pattern. Therefore, if this model is correct, deviations from linearity, to a first approximation, should lead to a reduction in the detectability of the pattern purely on the basis of the reduced height of the increased number of autocorrelogram peaks.

How, then, do we account for the continued decline in the detectability of the patterns as the deviation from linearity increases although the number of dots remains constant? The answer lies in understanding what happens to the autocorrelogram as the stimulus continues to deviate from linearity. Figures 3-5c and d show that the peaks in the autocorrelogram become more widely spaced as the angle becomes more acute.* This particular case, indeed, is the source of the original suggestion that a Pythagorean correction factor must be included in the expression for the figure of merit. No matter what the exact formularization of the best fitting figure of merit turns out to be, the conjecture is that the increased spacing between the peaks in the autocorrelogram is closely associated with the reduction in detectability of stimuli with increased angularity or curvature. This holds true even when the dot spacings in the original stimulus patterns are held constant. In any event, it can also be noted that the decrease

---

* This is one of the cases in which the changing line orientation has produced a greater distance between the dots of the simulated stimuli used in the autocorrelation. However, an earlier autocorrelogram using an optical autocorrelator (Uttal, 1973b) showed this increase in peak separation even when the artifact was not present. The additional effect caused by the coarseness of the grid is therefore only a quantitative and not a qualitative change and does not affect the general conclusions of the comparison.

V. TESTS OF THE MODEL

in detectability in the corresponding psychophysical experiment is matched by the decrease in the figures of merit of the autocorrelations of the four simulated stimulus patterns.

The very strong dependence of detectability on the regularity of dot spacing was the original observation compelling consideration of the autocorrelation transform as a possible model for this form of pattern detection. It is therefore especially interesting to consider the effect of dot spacing irregularity on the figures of merit. Figure 3-6 is a collection of three autocorrelograms, each of which is the transform of a straight line of a constant length composed of five collinear dots. However, the three dotted lines exhibit varying degrees of spacing irregularity, from a perfectly regular line to lines in which one or two dots are displaced along the axis. The variation in dot regularity appears to produce changes in the figure of merit for each pattern that correspond to the results of the analogous psychophysical Experiment IV. The regular line displays a higher figure of merit than do the two irregular lines, just as the regular stimuli are more easily detected than the irregular stimuli.

Next, consider the situation of transverse, instead of collinear, deviations from linearity. Figure 3-7 consists of four simulated stimuli and their autocorrelograms that are analogous to the transversely displaced stimuli of Experiment V. One of the autocorrelograms is of a five-dot line that is perfectly straight and evenly spaced; one is of a similar line but with one dot transversely displaced one grid unit; one is of a line with one dot transversely displaced two grid units; one is of a line with two dots transversely displaced two and one grid units, respectively. These four patterns, therefore, present a graded series of lines of progressively greater transverse displacement. Comparison of the four test patterns shows a progressive decline in the figures of merit as the magnitude of the displacement increases. The expression for deviation [Eq. (2-1)] was used in this case to order the variation of these figures. Again, the ordering of the figures of merit as a function of transverse irregularity corresponds to the ordering of stimulus detectability in the psychophysical experiment.

A further test, the first to involve polygons, dealt with the mutilated triangle patterns of Experiment VI. This experiment proved to be of especial psychophysical interest in that the results obtained were

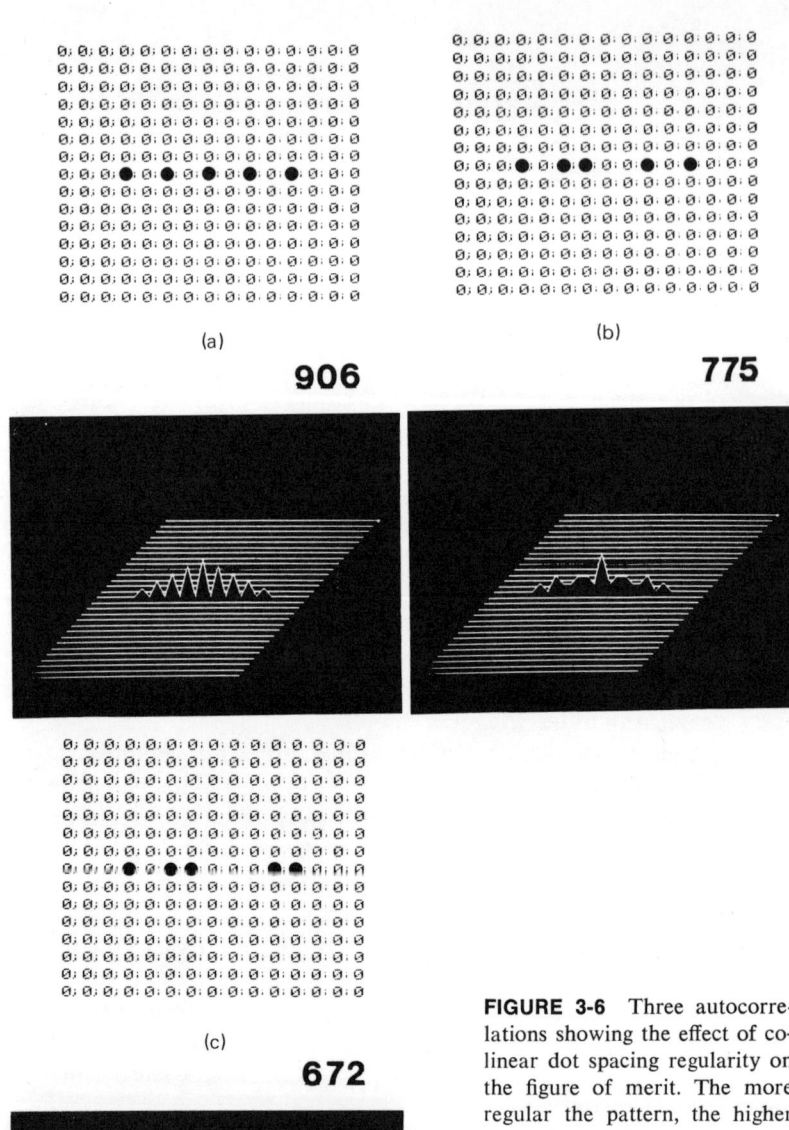

FIGURE 3-6 Three autocorrelations showing the effect of colinear dot spacing regularity on the figure of merit. The more regular the pattern, the higher is the figure of merit.

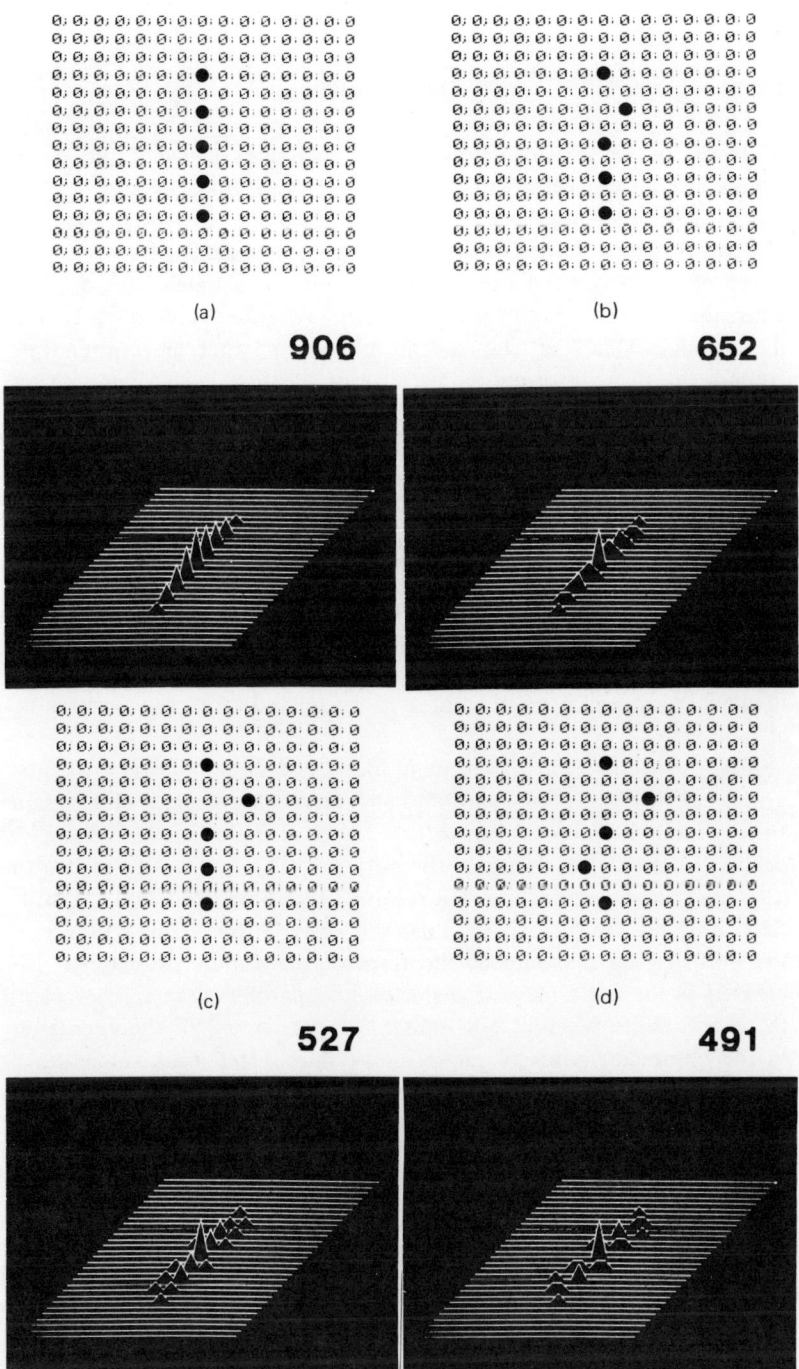

FIGURE 3-7 Four autocorrelations showing the effect of transverse dot spacing regularity on the figure of merit. The greater the deviation from regularity, the lower is the figure of merit.

contrary to our a priori and intuitive estimates of what the effect would be. It was observed in Experiment VI that, as expected, a complete triangle was more detectable than one in which some of the constituent dots had been removed. Unexpectedly, however, the effect of removing the dots from the sides was much greater than when the same number of dots was removed either randomly or from the corners. This was true in spite of the fact that the corner dots contain the most information because of the reduced redundancy of the pattern in the corners.

The results of the simulation test are shown in Figure 3-8. In accord with the psychophysical experiment, the complete triangle has the highest figure of merit, the pattern with only three dots in each side has a lower one, and the patterns composed only of corner dots or those patterns that remain after random dot deletions have similar but even lower figures of merit. The proposed autocorrelation model, in this case, again adequately predicts the psychophysical findings. When the sides are disrupted, the decline in detectability is greater than when an equal number of dots is deleted from the corners or at random.

The psychophysical experiment that examined the effect of progressive distortions of a square into an increasingly acute parallelogram showed that the increased distortion led to a modest, but monotonic, decline in the detectability of the patterns. The figures of merit also displayed a modest decline as a result of the same distortion of simulated stimuli. Unfortunately, this was one of those cases in which the dot spacing of some of the lines of the simulated patterns increased as the patterns were distorted into parallelograms. Therefore, there was some residual possibility that part or all of the reduction in the obtained figures of merit of the autocorrelogram might have been caused by increasing dot spacing. Although the changes in the figure of merit predicted by the model did correspond to the psychophysical data, this artifact negated the utility of this test, and these autocorrelograms will not be presented.

Experiment IX, dealing with the effects of the degree of organization of several straight-line segments, introduces another important set of issues. The general result of the psychophysical experiment indicated that the organization, in general, of the line segments into any pattern led to an increase in detectability. The results of the test

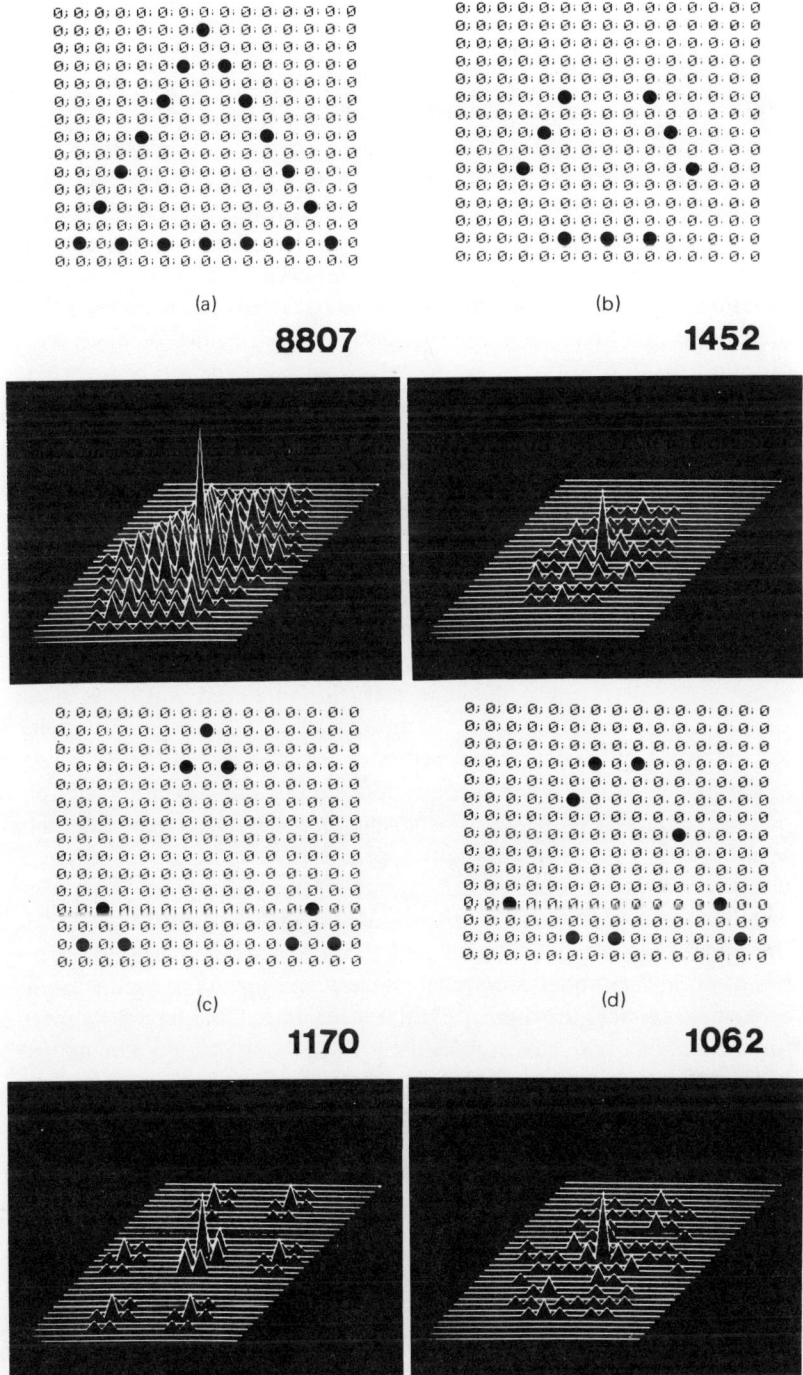

FIGURE 3-8 Four autocorrelations showing the effect of mutilating triangles on the figure of merit. A whole triangle (a) has the highest figure of merit; a triangle composed only of sides (b) has the next highest; and both corners (c) and random deletions (d) have similar, but lower, figures of merit.

of the autocorrelation model are shown in Figure 3-9 for the three line-segment version and in Figure 3-10 for the four line-segment version. In each case, the first pattern to be autocorrelated mimics the random "pick-up-sticks" stimulus, whereas the other simulated stimuli have been composed of these same segments arranged in an orderly fashion. The simulation model produces figures of merit with ordering that corresponds to the psychophysical data; the irregular pattern autocorrelations display lower figures of merit than do those of the regular patterns.

However, the figures of merit of the autocorrelations of the regular patterns did not cluster together as the psychophysical detectability scores did. Although the differences among the figures of merit were understandable in terms of the geometry of the patterns (more regular spacing of the line segments led invariably to higher figures of merit), a question remained concerning the lack of correspondence between the almost constant psychophysical results for the regular patterns and the varying figures of merit for simulations of those same stimuli. Unfortunately, the psychophysical data were sufficiently noisy to preclude a judgment as to whether or not this sort of fine structure in the figures of merit was actually reflected in the perceptual performance. Although there was no reason to either expect or require a linear relation between the figures of merit and the psychophysical data, it would be interesting, in some future study, to determine whether the model would also work at this microstructural level. For the moment, however, even though the major ordering has been reproduced in the model, we are left with what appears to be a second-order discrepancy, for there are differences among the figures of merit for the regular patterns produced by the model that do not appear to be reflected in the psychophysical data.

Speculation about the source of this discrepancy suggests several possible explanations. The model itself is possibly the source of the discrepancy. It may introduce additional variation in the figure of merit because of some biologically unrealizable aspect of the mathematics used in its development, a common enough problem in such sciences as the physics of quanta. In some instances in quantum mechanics, certain of the complex roots of a mathematical formularization must simply be rejected; they are of no physical significance and are merely superfluous features of the utilized mathematics. The

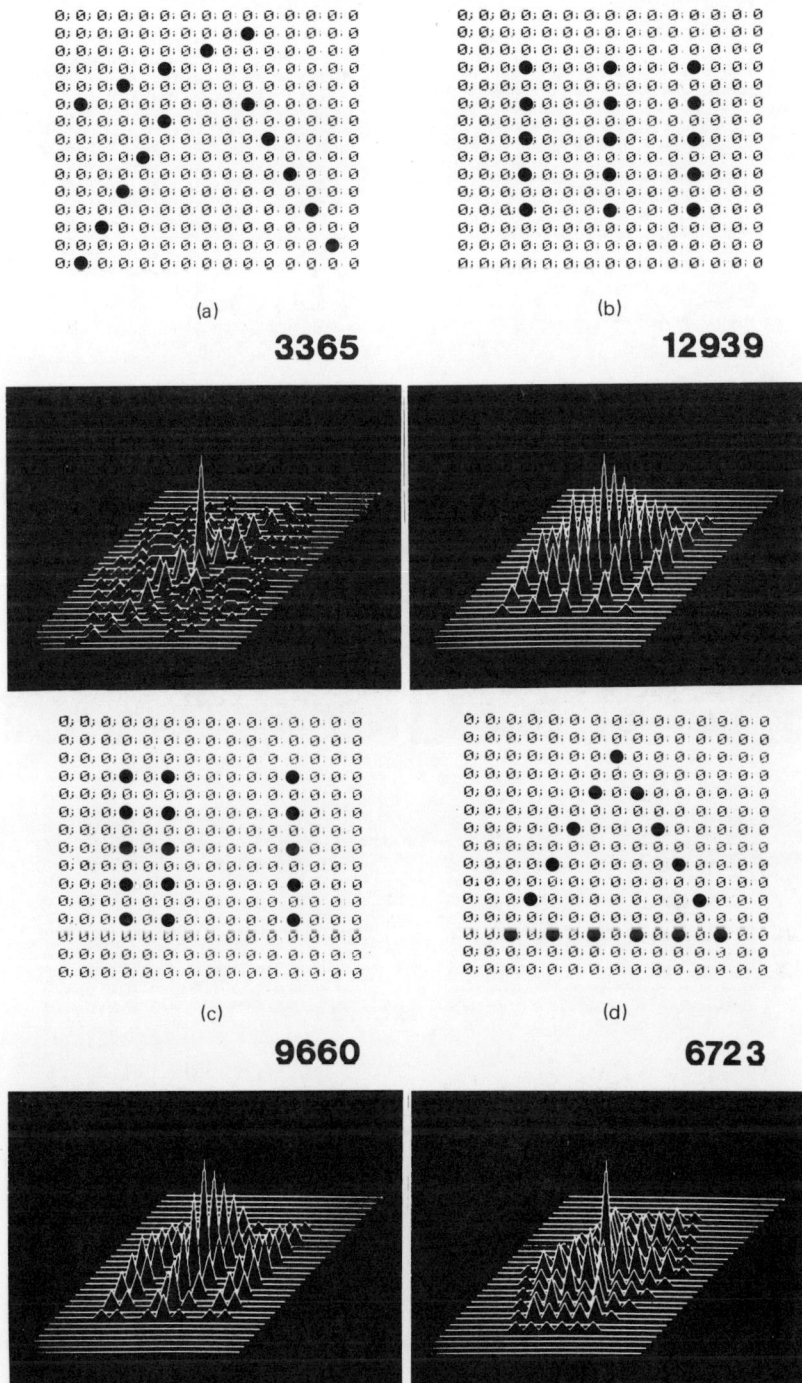

FIGURE 3-9 Four autocorrelations showing the effect of organizing three line segments into various regular patterns on the figure of merit. The pick-up-sticks pattern (a) has a substantially lower figure of merit than the three other, more regular patterns.

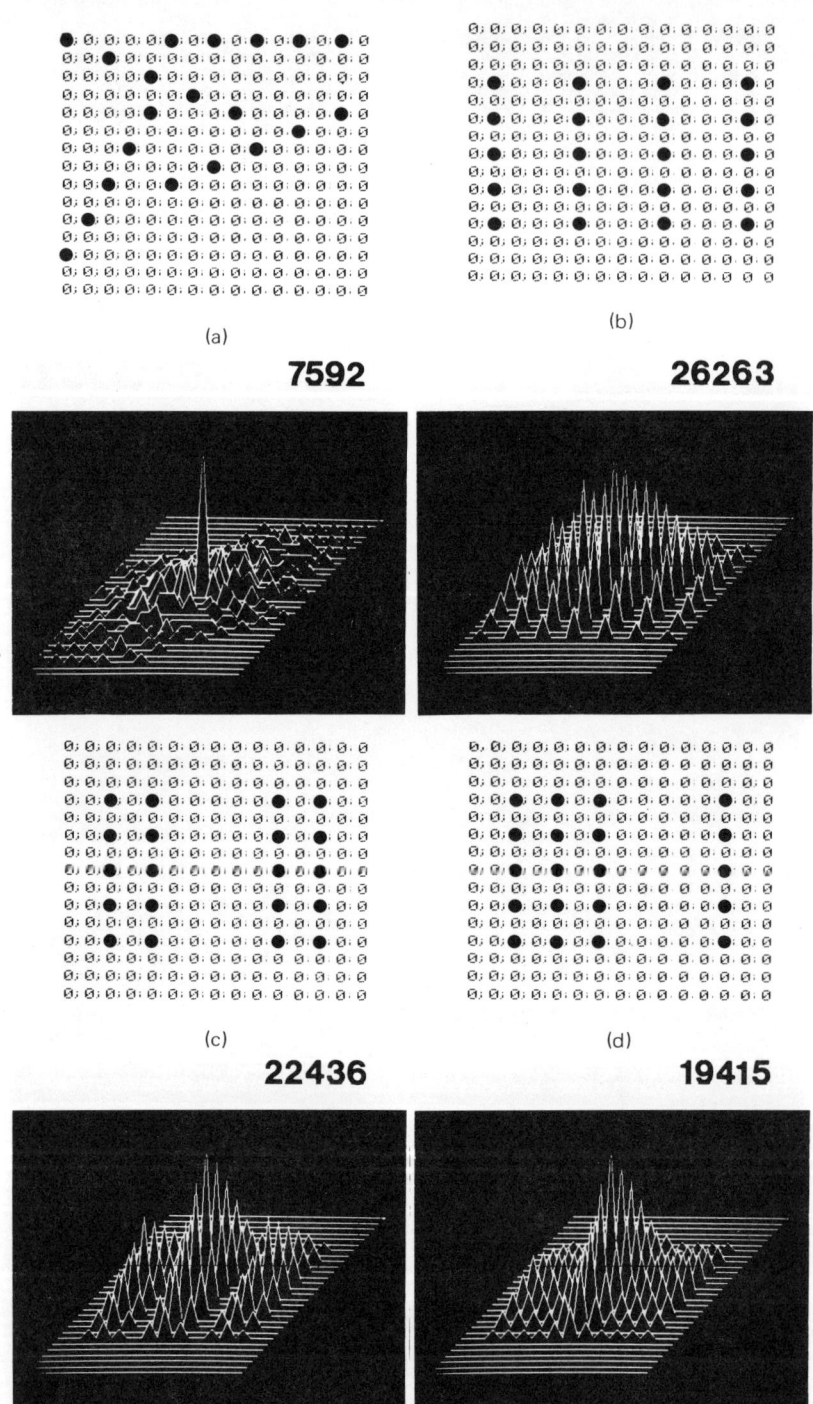

FIGURE 3-10a–d

V. TESTS OF THE MODEL

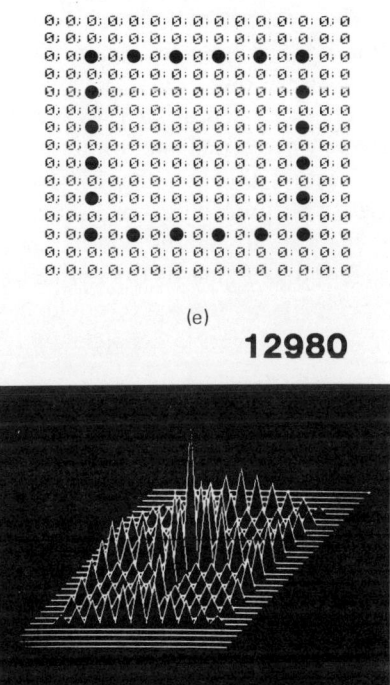

(e)

FIGURE 3-10 Five autocorrelograms showing the effect of organizing four line segments into various regular patterns on the figure of merit. The pick-up-sticks pattern (a) has a substantially lower figure of merit than the four more regular patterns.

FIGURE 3-10c

expression [Eq. (3-1)] used for the figure of merit in the present model, however, may be too sensitive to aspects of the stimuli that the human observer ordinarily ignores. For example, the model may reflect a sensitivity to line spacing regularity that is not evidenced in the psychophysical findings.

A second possibility is some insensitivity on the part of the autocorrelation to aspects of the stimulus to which the human responds. It is also possible that the discrepancy between the figures of merit and the psychophysical data may simply be caused by noise or sampling errors in the psychophysical data. The microstructure simply may not show in this experiment. In any event, no other formularization for the figure of merit, among the several tried, does better in accounting for the major effects. These secondary discrepancies must therefore be tolerated for the time being.

The next set of tests of the model dealt with the analogs of the stimuli of Experiment X. In these tests, corners of squares and triangles were displaced from perfect regularity in order to determine the effects of figural integrity on detectability. This set of autocorrelograms was carried out with simulated stimuli plotted on a 20×20 grid rather than on the 15×15 grid used in all of the preceding tests. This procedure was required to help keep the center of gravity of the various figures approximately constant. With figures such as these, moving one of the corners closer to or farther away from the other parts of the figure could have artificially altered the value of the figure of merit independently of any changes produced by varying the organization of the stimuli.

Figure 3-11 shows the effects of the displacement of the corners of a triangle on its autocorrelograms and figures of merit. Displacing one or two corners leads to a progressive decline in the figure of merit in much the same way that the original stimulus patterns decline in psychophysical detectability when the real stimulus corners are shifted. Finally, a greatly reduced figure of merit is produced by a single corner, again corresponding to the low detectability of such a stimulus in the psychophysical experiments.

Figures 3-12, 3-13, and 3-14 present the results of the more elaborate test for patterns composed of the four corners of a square. First, Figure 3-12 shows the progressive effect of the displacement of corners as the patterns vary from a perfect square to a square with one disarranged corner, to a square with two disarranged corners, and, finally, to a square with randomly placed corners. The figures of merit again decline in the same order as the psychophysical detectability scores for similar stimuli. Figure 3-13 then shows the effects of autocorrelating analogs of other parts of the original experiment that have varied the number of 90° corners present in the stimulus. Finally, Figure 3-14 shows the test pattern and autocorrelation resulting when the same four corners of a square are arranged in an entirely different pattern, the staircase. The figure of merit for this arrangement is also high, just as its detectability is high in the psychophysical experiment.

Experiment XI dealt with the effect of the "goodness" of the stimulus patterns that was metricized by Garner and Clement (1963). Their study employed several tasks to assess the degree to which figural goodness was an effective determinant of performance. Our

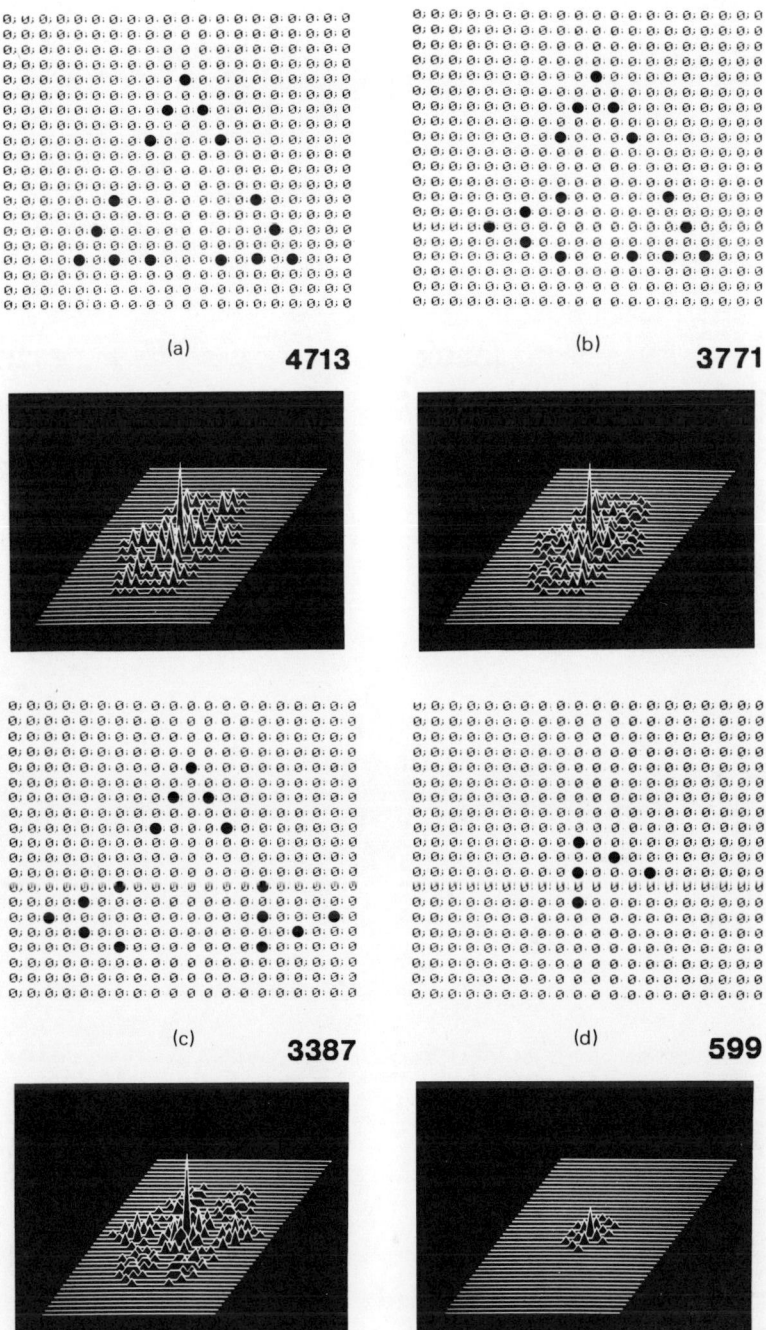

FIGURE 3-11 Four autocorrelations showing the effect of disorganizing the corners of triangles on the figure of merit. The greater the disorganization, the lower is the figure of merit. Also a single corner (d) has a very low figure of merit.

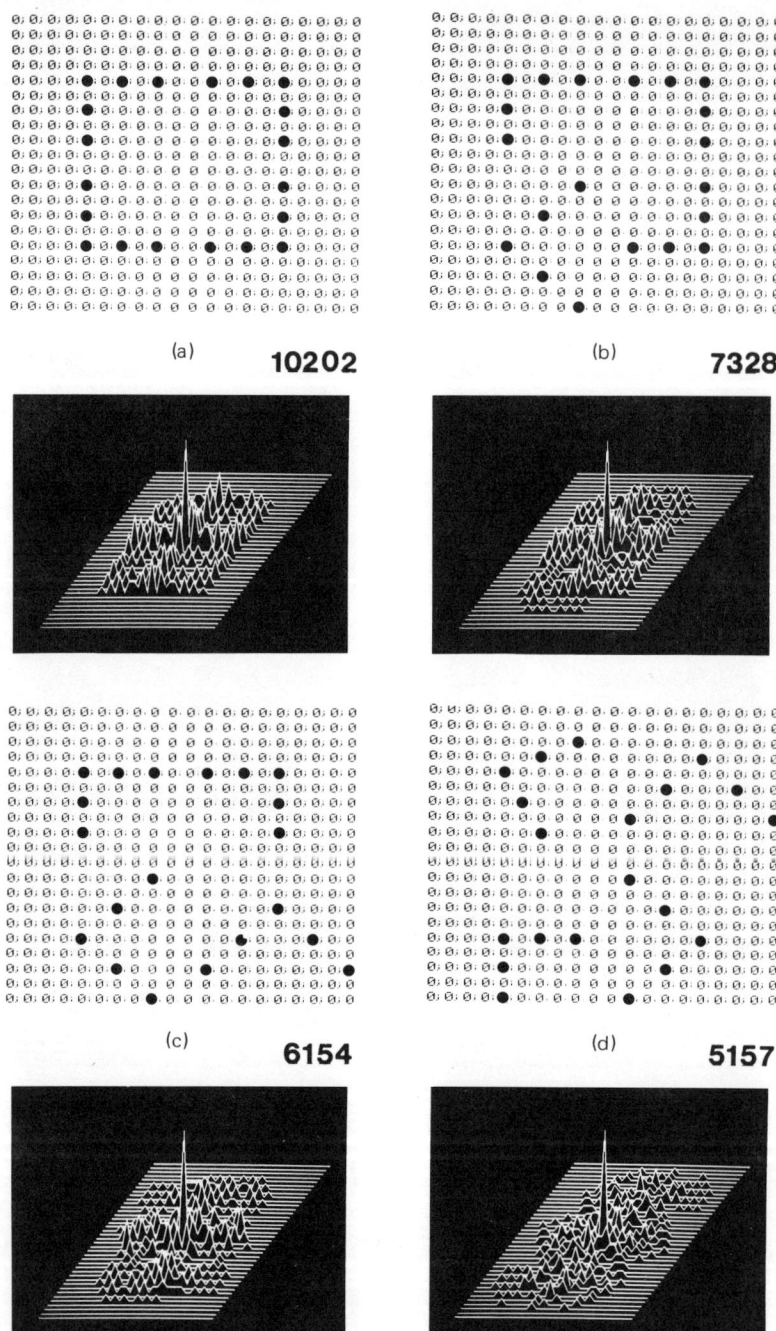

FIGURE 3-12 Four autocorrelations showing the effects of disorganizing the corners of a square on the figure of merit. The greater the disorganization, the lower is the figure of merit.

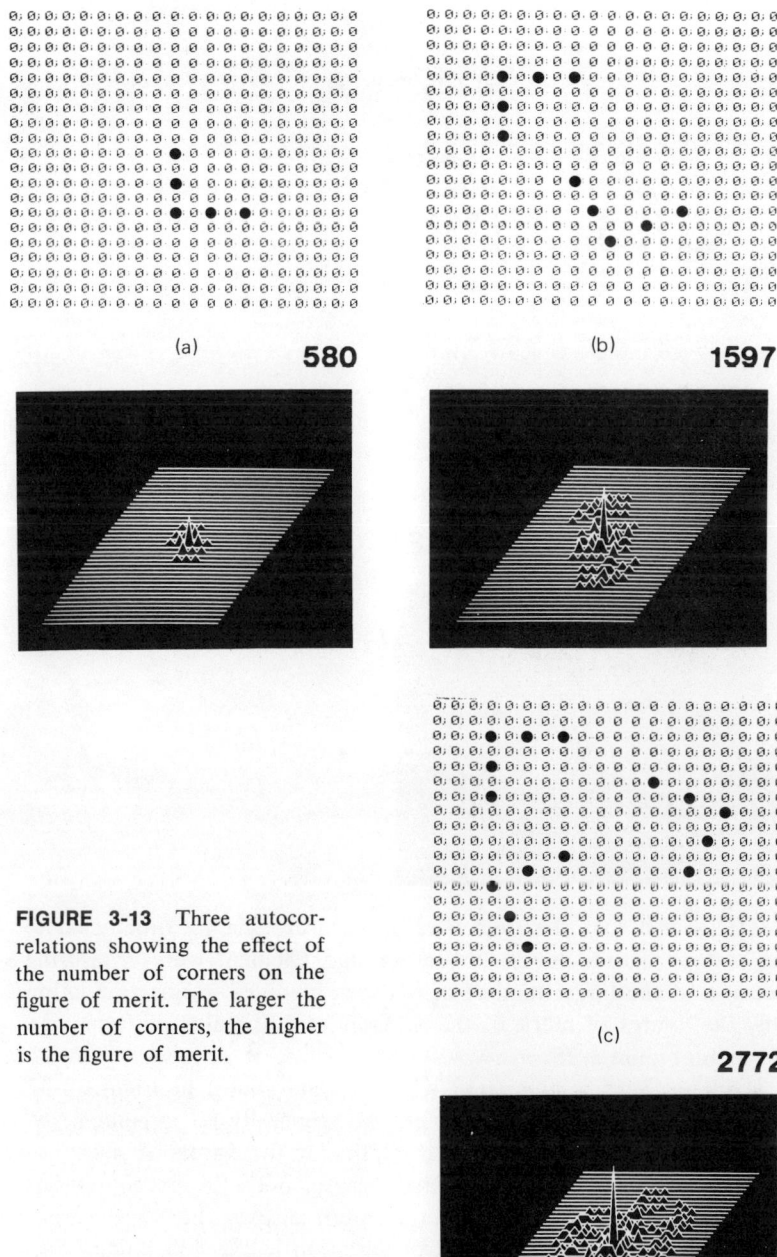

FIGURE 3-13 Three autocorrelations showing the effect of the number of corners on the figure of merit. The larger the number of corners, the higher is the figure of merit.

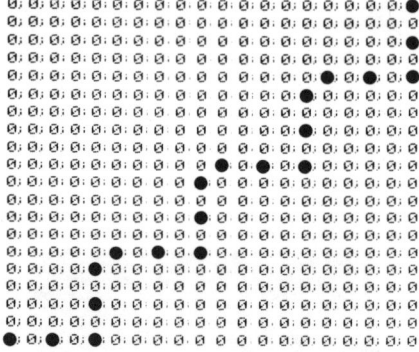

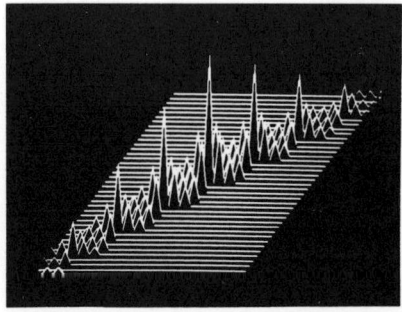

FIGURE 3-14 An autocorrelation showing the high figure of merit obtained with another regular four-corner pattern, a staircase arrangement.

study showed that the detection scores were mainly unaffected by the sort of figural goodness Garner and Clement were measuring. Because of the large number of patterns involved in our simulation, only the figures of merit of the 18 simulated stimulus patterns were plotted in Figure 3-15.

If Figure 3-15 is compared with the data shown in Figure 2-32, it can be seen that the two graphs are generally in agreement. No major decline in either the detectability or the figure of merit can be observed in either figure. Furthermore, both the psychophysical data and the plot of the figures of merit display the same general pattern: a considerable amount of variation in the first half of each curve between adjacent patterns and a subsequent settling out later in the series. The major discrepancies that prevent the curves from fitting almost perfectly are few. The figure of merit is too low for

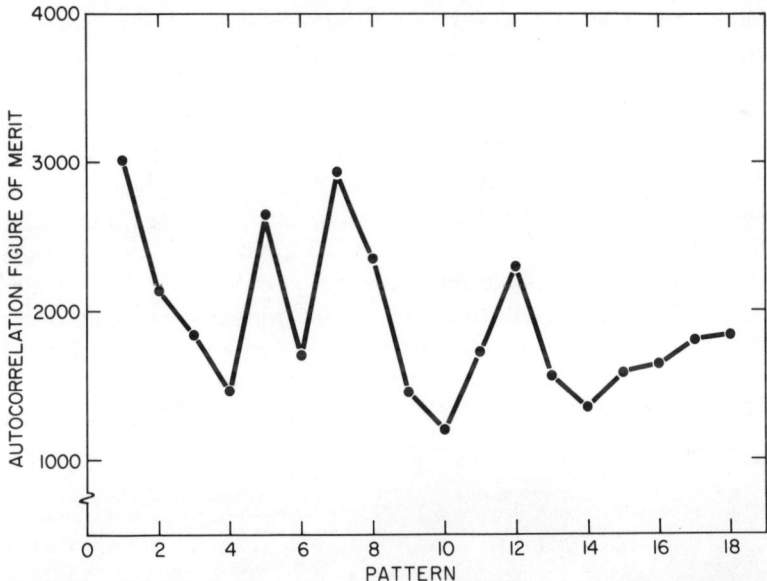

FIGURE 3-15 Graph showing the figures of merit obtained by autocorrelating patterns similar to those used by Garner and Clement (1963). This figure should be compared to Fig. 2-32 to see that the pattern is generally the same. There is no major decline in the figures of merit as the figural "goodness" dimension is scanned. The variability observed between the figures of merit of adjacent targets in the first part of the graph is reduced in the second part; the same pattern is observed in the psychophysical data.

Patterns 3 and 6 and too high for Pattern 8, compared to the psychophysical data.

The general correspondence between the psychophysical results and the autocorrelation is robust, in spite of these few discrepancies. As in the psychophysical data, the overall trend of the curve of autocorrelations is generally flat, in spite of the strong variation in ranked goodness obtained in Garner and Clement's experiment. Clearly, the dimension that these investigators have metricized neither affects the detectability that is assayed by the dot-masking paradigm to any great degree nor systematically affects the figures of merit of the autocorrelated simulated stimuli. The discrepancies between the output of the model and the psychophysical data, however, reflect the same difficulty encountered earlier in this discussion of the model—most likely caused either by the inadequacy of the expression for the figure of merit or by sampling errors or noise in the psychophysical data.

Now, to tackle another issue, it is well known that in order to mimic human performance, an artificial pattern recognition system must possess a minimal sensitivity to translation and rotation. Although an experiment with dot patterns (Uttal, 1972) dealing specifically with translation has been previously carried out, the translations examined in that study vary only over a narrow range. No good evidence is at hand for the effect of translation over wide ranges. Therefore, the following simulation test dealing with the sensitivity of the model to translation is presented ad hoc, simply to demonstrate this aspect of the design of the computer program. Figure 3-16 shows the simulated stimuli, autocorrelograms, and figures of merit for two

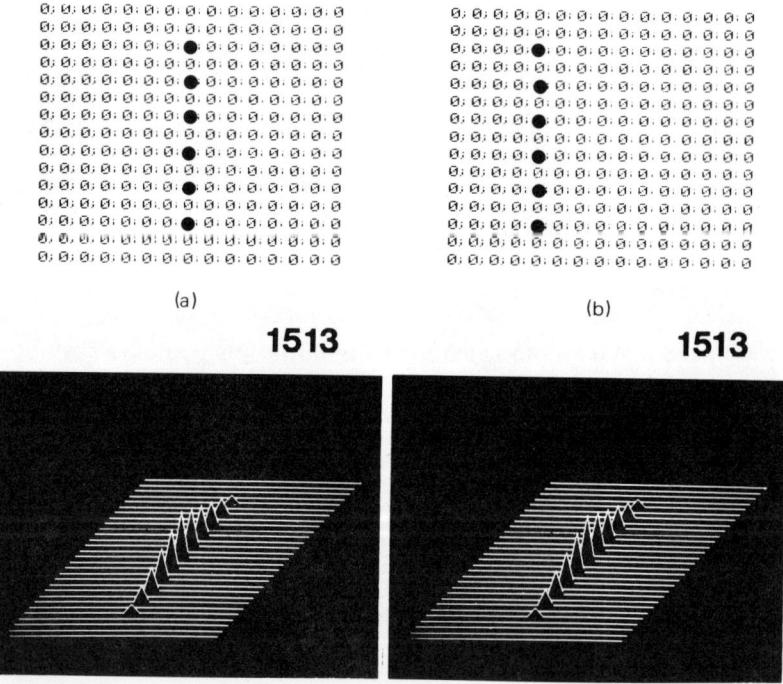

FIGURE 3-16 Two autocorrelations showing the absence of any effect of position or translation on the figure of merit for a straight line.

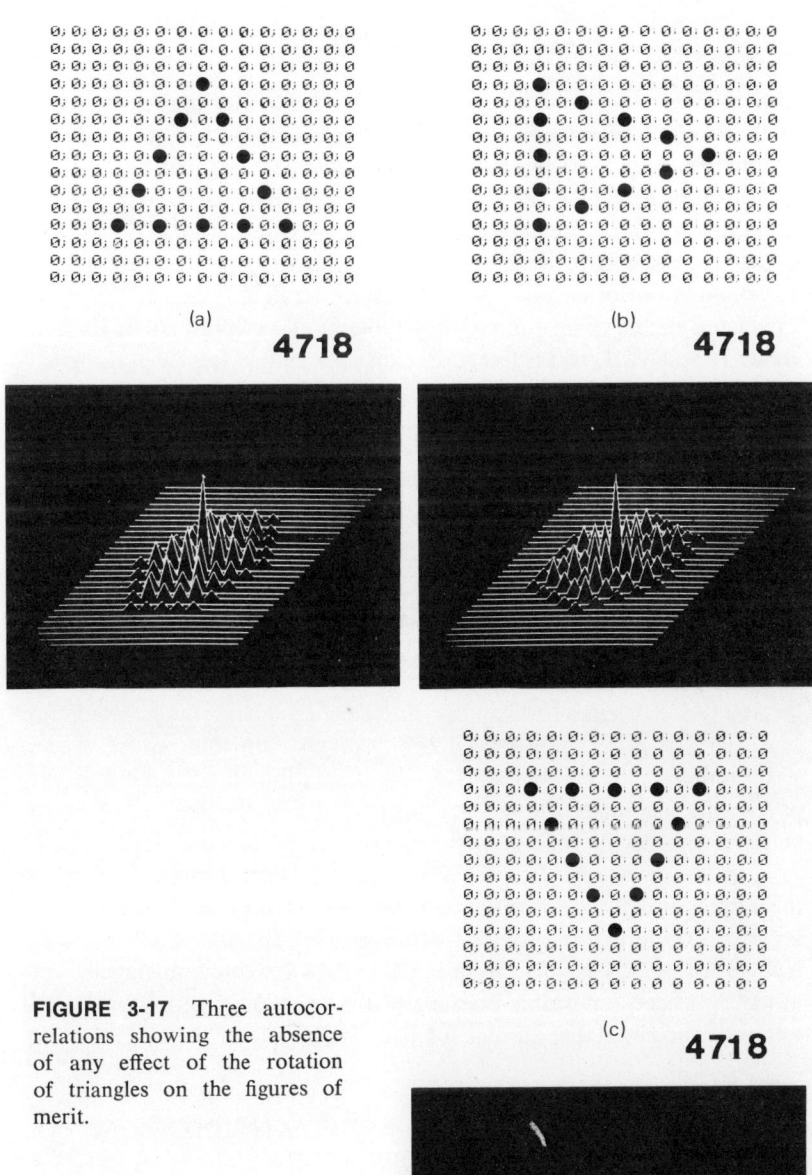

FIGURE 3-17 Three autocorrelations showing the absence of any effect of the rotation of triangles on the figures of merit.

straight lines that differ only in their position. The figures of merit of the two autocorrelograms are identical. Obviously, the model is in agreement with the psychophysical data in this regard.

However, a test of sensitivity of the model to rotation is not as straightforward as the test of the effect of translation. The experiments discussed here have convincingly shown that the dot-masking paradigm is not orientation sensitive. Both straight lines and polygons have been shown to be equally detectable at all orientations in Experiments II and VIII, respectively. Because the model has been designed to be specific to this dot-masking situation, it should also reflect this same insensitivity to orientation. Figure 3-17 shows that this is exactly the obtained result for triangular patterns of varying orientations. However, because of the coarse grid of the field on which the simulated stimulus patterns have been introduced into the computer, varying the orientation of dotted straight lines or squares to obliqueness would change the actual Pythagorean distance between the dots of the test pattern. This artifact makes it impossible to test the model for orientation effects with these kinds of stimuli. Nonetheless, by now the reader should be sufficiently familiar with the technique to be assured that, if a sufficiently fine-grained matrix were used, no sensitivity to orientation would be observed with this model.

In summary, a comparison of the simulation test results and the psychophysical data shows agreement between the figures of merit and the psychophysical data for nearly all of the dimensions considered in this study. In two cases, discrepancies obtained between the model and the psychophysical data have probably resulted from an inappropriate form for the expression of the figure of merit or from noise in the psychophysical data. In a few other instances, the model has been untestable because of the coarseness of the grid used to define the simulated stimuli for the autocorrelator.

VI. SPECULATIONS ON A NEUROPHYSIOLOGICAL AUTOCORRELATOR

The model of visual pattern perception involving autocorrelation transforms that has so far been described and tested should be embodied in some kind of neural network if it is to have any realistic

VI. SPECULATIONS ON A NEUROPHYSIOLOGICAL AUTOCORRELATOR

substance and applicability to the biological process it represents. The next question asked therefore concerns the plausibility of the model in the context of contemporary neurophysiology.

The autocorrelation transform, as embodied in the expression of Eq. (1-1), may be conceived of as consisting of a sequence of mathematical operations. It is necessary to sequentially carry out a number of steps to autocorrelate a stimulus pattern:

1. Provide a set of replicas of the form $f(x + \Delta x, y + \Delta y)$ by some kind of shifting operation on the original stimulus $f(x, y)$.
2. Cross-multiply each of the replicas by the original stimulus for each point in the visual field.
3. Summate or integrate all of the cross products to give a value of the integral for each $\Delta x, \Delta y$ shift.
4. Plot all of the integrals of Step 3 in the $\Delta x, \Delta y$ space to form the entire autocorrelation function.

None of these operations is difficult to construct from the simplest type of hypothetical neural interactions. As one example of a network that would carry out a process analogous to the autocorrelation transform, consider Figure 3-18. This diagrammatic sketch of a hypothetical neural network invokes nothing beyond the most plausible neural mechanisms. Indeed, only a few well-known characteristics of neural interconnection are required to implement a structure that will certainly be capable of performing the autocorrelation transform.

The first operation that might be performed is the construction of the set of shifted replicas. In a serial processing computer, this operation is considerably more difficult than in the parallel processing nerve net of Figure 3-18. In the parallel nerve net, all that is required to produce the shifted replicas is a set of laterally conducting connectives to convey information about one part of the stimulus space to other locations. For example, in this figure, the stimulus pattern in the external x, y space has been assumed to be a row of uniformly spaced dots. The information pattern is initially encoded in what must be at least a topologically constant, if not isomorphic, representation by the visual receptor; it is then conveyed to some more central locus in the nervous system, remaining in that same spatially encoded form.

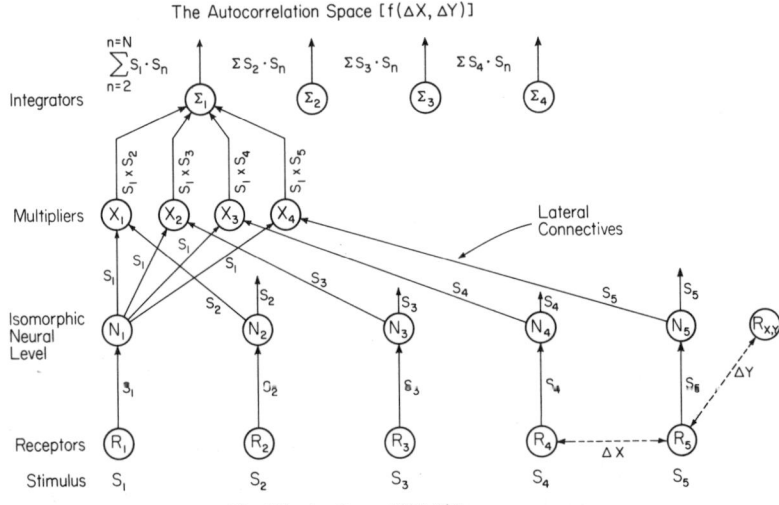

FIGURE 3-18 Schematic drawing of a hypothetical, but plausible, neural information-processing net that could produce the autocorrelation transform. Stimulus patterns are transformed from the (x, y) space at the bottom of the figure to the $(\Delta x, \Delta y)$ space at the top by simple neural interconnections. The neural "units" indicated may be single cells or more complex subunits. The figure is presented only to show the relative ease with which a neural autocorrelator can be implemented.

We shall refer to this locus as the isomorphic (stretching the definition of isomorphism only slightly) neural level but shall not specify its exact location other than to say that it is probably central.

Satisfactory analogs of shifted replicas, which overlap with the isomorphic representation of the original stimulus, are immediately available simply as a consequence of the function of the lateral connections between different portions of the isomorphic neural levels. Therefore, if the units (labeled N_n) in Fig. 3-18 at the isomorphic level send coded signals to a series of multipliers (labeled X_n) on both direct and collateral lines, then each of the multipliers receives inputs corresponding to the parts of the stimulus immediately below it as well as to parts at distant locations (i.e., the shifted replicas).

The "multipliers" or some equivalent repetitive summators can be implemented simply by concatenating a number of excitatory inputs

VI. SPECULATIONS ON A NEUROPHYSIOLOGICAL AUTOCORRELATOR

by means of simple convergent summation. The output of these neural multipliers can then be considered to be exact equivalents of the cross products of $f(x, y)$ and $f(x + \Delta x, y + \Delta y)$ that have been generated in the computer simulation of the model. Those cross products that represent lateral displacements equivalent to the periodic wavelength of the stimulus pattern have a high value, whereas those that do not match the periodic properties of the input pattern produce low values.

Integration, or, more properly in this discrete neural information processor, a summation that is not carried to the infinitesimal limit, is also directly and easily implemented by simple convergent summative inputs. Multiple graded signals convergently impinging on the dendrites of a given neuron may produce a continuously graded output signal or, coded with another neural dimension, may affect the firing frequency of a spike action potential in direct proportion to the integrated values of the several inputs. The output of one such convergent integrator, then, is the equivalent of the autocorrelation integral of Eq. (1-1) for a particular $\Delta x, \Delta y$ value. The output of the entire family of such units represents the total autocorrelation surface over the entire $\Delta x, \Delta y$ space.

A similar exercise in this kind of spatial, neurophysiological "mathematics" can be carried out to implement the expression for the figure of merit, but this is probably not necessary; the figure of merit is more of a convenience to the modeler than a necessary feature of the brain. It is entirely reasonable to expect that the global brain state defined at the outputs of the family of convergent integrators is a valid "figure of merit" as it stands. In other words, the global brain state itself is tantamount, in such a parallel processing net, to the "value" of the autocorrelogram. On a molar level, the human is able to deal simultaneously with so few bits of information that he is essentially acting as a serial information processor. Molar "psychological bits," therefore, cannot be considered to be equivalent to the "microbits" of the nervous system. For this reason, the expression for the figure of merit is needed to assist the experimenter in his evaluation and comparison of the autocorrelograms.

The final physiological question of consequence concerns the locus in the nervous system at which such an autocorrelation mechanism may be placed. The total impact of the present study supports an explanation based on interactions that occur among points in a stimulus space that are still at least topologically isomorphic with the external world. This means that the processes being considered here are occurring before any reencoding of the stimulus into nonisomorphic representations. Therefore, the suggestion is that the neural autocorrelation process represented by this model occurs relatively early in the cortical network, possibly quite soon after the primary or secondary visual areas where isomorphic representation is still present. Beyond these general speculations on the locus of the autocorrelator, no data are available that permit a more specific statement.

4
Summary—An Alternative Neural Implementation

Theoretical attempts to account for cognitive functions have challenged psychobiologists for a considerable time. Only in the sensory and perceptual domain, however, is there sufficient simplicity of structure and organization of descriptive concepts of the process to allow neural modeling to progress. A large number of alternatives have been considered, only a few of which have been reviewed in Chapter 1. Some of them are based on specific assumptions concerning the physiology of individual neurons, whereas others emphasize the network properties of the nervous system. In the following summary, a few of the most important contemporary theories are reviewed and an attempt is made to place the autocorrelation hypothesis in context with them.

The attribution by psychobiologists of global pattern detection properties to single neural units tuned to particular forms is, of course, based on the distinguished neurophysiological contributions of such workers as Hubel and Wiesel (1968), Barlow and Levick (1965), Lettvin, Maturana, McCulloch, and Pitts (1959), and Whitfield and Evans (1965). All of these investigators have shown that individual neurons located at various levels of the ascending sensory pathways are capable of selectively responding to stimuli that have particular "triggers" sensitive to specific spatial and temporal features of the stimulus. Psychobiological theorists have noted a number of analogies that exist between these neurophysiological data and what, at first glance, appear to be corresponding psychophysical phenomena. A wide variety of perceptual phenomena, including such dramatic effects as grid adaptation, color effects, and spatial illusions, has been attributed to the action (or inaction in the case of experiments that involve adaptive suppression) of units with analogous specificity.

Theories oriented toward some form of Fourier analysis (see, for example, Pollen, Lee, & Taylor, 1971), however, suggest that many similar processes are affected in a way that can be best explained on the basis of increasing or decreasing specific sensitivities to spatial frequencies. The diminishment in perceptual sensitivity to the contrast of gratings of the same spatial frequency as those in an adapting field, for example, has been attributed to the adaptation of spatial frequency-specific neurons in the cat's striate cortex by Maffei, Fiorentini, and Bisti (1973). (This study is particularly interesting because it is one of the few to report a correspondence between the time scales of the neural and perceptual processes.)

Those theories which assume, without specific neurophysiologic modeling that a particular form of information processing underlies pattern recognition are at another level of conceptual discourse. Comparisons of stimulus patterns to a stored set of templates (a cross-correlational approach) or to local or global density determinations have been invoked as possible mechanisms capable of explaining similar perceptual phenomena.

The present theoretical presentation has many points in common with all of these models. It deals with a relatively specific, although hypothetical, neural structure arranged as a computational network

SUMMARY—AN ALTERNATIVE NEURAL IMPLEMENTATION

the antecedents of which are clearly of the class mentioned above. However, it also assumes certain premises that are special to the autocorrelation approach and minimizes a number of the difficulties that some of these other theories inject into any consideration of the possible physiological mechanisms of pattern recognition.

The earlier sections of this study described a mathematical model based on such a hypothetical neural autocorrelation mechanism of a particular form of pattern recognition—a paradigm that involved dotted-pattern detection in dotted visual noise. A series of psychophysical experiments was carried out and the results compared with autocorrelations of simulated approximations to the psychophysical stimulus patterns. A satisfactory correspondence was found between the simulated autocorrelations (as metricized by an arbitrary figure of merit) and the psychophysical data.

Although the fit between the empirical data and the theory is not perfect, it is clear that even the modest success of this comparison raises a fundamental issue with regard to theoretical models of form perception. The autocorrelation model differs, with regard to its implementation, in a number of important ways from many of the theories that have wider currency in contemporary psychobiology. If one were to build an autocorrelator, the mechanical device produced would be quite different than if one were to build a feature filter. This is the aspect referred to as the neural implementation, and it is one of the more fundamental ways in which these models differ.

However dissimilar the various theories may be in terms of the biological processes that underlie them, it must also be remembered that there is a formal equivalence among many of the mathematical formularizations associated with each approach. For example, as mentioned previously, if it can be shown that an autocorrelation model can work well in predicting the psychophysical data, it is a necessary consequence that an alternative mathematical model involving spatial frequency analysis is also possible and that it probably works just as well. This is true because the autocorrelation and the power spectrum density of any function are related; the Fourier transform of the autocorrelation must be the same as the independently arrived at power spectrum density, and vice versa. The same amount of information is lost with either process and the same properties, therefore, remain for evaluation, even though they may be in a different mathematical form after the respective transformations.

In view of this formal identity, it must be kept clearly in mind that it is the concept of a spatially distributed neural mechanism composed of unspecialized neurons that is the main thesis of this model, not the fact that this or any other single mathematical formularization is unique or superior to any other. Indeed, the discrepancies that exist bear testimony to the fact that the proposed formularization is not yet perfect and that some other similar model, more or less sensitive to other attributes of the stimulus, may provide a better fit. However, the notion of the algorithmic, parallel-processing autocorrelator is as distinct in neurophysiological detail from the feature filter approaches, whether specific feature- or spatial frequency-sensitive, as it is from the template comparing cross correlators and other similar information-processing models.

Even within the limited context of an autocorrelation theory, however, there is great uncertainty about the exact form that the function should take. The form of the autocorrelation function that we have chosen is based on the Cartesian coordinate system and is thus constrained to a rectangular grid and constant spacing. There is no reason why this should be the case in the visual system. A polar coordinate embodiment of the autocorrelation function might have provided a better fit between the psychophysical data and the mathematical model. Similarly, an autocorrelation function that was based upon a different, and perhaps even an anisotropic, spacing metric might have been preferable. Oyama,[*] in a personal communication, has suggested that spacing metrics based on logarithmic steps or even on constant cortical spacing might be much more effective in predicting the psychophysical data.

Whatever the form, it is clear that all mathematical theories of form perception share a common disadvantage because they are based mainly on the kind of input–output analysis that is characteristic of psychophysical experimentation. At present, no empirical means exist that enable selection of the unique or actual neural implementation from among the alternatives proposed by any of these theories. Much of the support for each theoretical approach comes from reasoning by analogy, criteria of parsimony, and judgments of scientific aesthet-

[*] Tadasu Oyama, Chiba University, Japan.

ics and elegance, as well as from a reasonable correspondence to the known physiological properties of very simple nerve nets. In all instances, each theory becomes speculative when it passes from the functionally descriptive issues to a discussion of specific structural properties. Therefore, the equivalences among the mathematical formularizations and the current constraint on our perspective, mainly to input–output arguments, always leave a residue of disappointment with even the most elegantly stated theory.

The direct proof, so desired, for one or another of the models of pattern recognition has not yet been achieved, as it has been for some other problems in psychobiology. For example, the determination of the spectral absorption curves of the three photopigments of the primate and teleost fish retinas was a most notable and successful example of a direct resolution of a controversy between biological (structural) and mathematical (descriptive) models of a perceptual process. The situation in color vision theories before these direct measurements were attained was identical to the problem of evaluating the models of pattern recognition now under consideration. Heretofore, several alternative mathematical–descriptive models assumed, for reasons individually compelling to their respective authors, several different sets of spectral absorption fundamentals for the three pigments. This issue was completely resolved when Brown and Wald (1964) and Marks, Dobelle, and MacNichol (1964) showed by microspectrophotometrics exactly what the absorption spectrum of each pigment was.

It is not yet certain whether or not current technology or future technique will be able to resolve the controversy among the theories of pattern recognition as definitively as it has for retinal pigment absorption curves. It is entirely possible that we may never be able to simultaneously measure a sufficient number of the properties of the distributed nerve nets that most certainly are involved in even the simplest of these cognitive processes. Therefore, the controversy is unlikely to be resolved in the foreseeable future, and it is probably necessary to accept the fact that criteria of parsimony and elegance are likely to play primary roles indefinitely.

Before considering some of the similarities and dissimilarities of various models further, it should also be reemphasized that the autocorrelation model presented here is aimed at explaining a fairly specific form of pattern recognition. It deals with a geometry-sensitive process that operates on isomorphically encoded stimuli at a level prior to the point at which the stimulus pattern is converted into symbolic representations. It is clearly categorized as a Stage 3 process (see Figure 1-2), therefore, and it is only to this level that the following comments are directed. It is entirely possible, and indeed most likely, that the whole idea of a spatial neural autocorrelator does not pertain to higher cognitive levels involving nonisomorphic and symbolic encoding. At some level of the nervous system, where the categorization process presumably takes place, some much more complex mechanism, perhaps better described as a template matcher, may be a more appropriate neural information-processing model. Again, the reader is reminded that the emphasis in this study is entirely on the relatively early detection processes and that the experimental task does not pertain to any of the other levels of visual information processing.

What, then, are the special advantages of the autocorrelation model that make it a more satisfying explanation of this third stage of perceptual processing than any of the other models? Some of the advantages are fairly general and involve matters of first approximation to related human behavior. Others pertain to some of the conceptual weaknesses of competing theories. For example, a cross-correlation model of pattern recognition involves, by the definition of that model, some set of templates against which the incoming stimuli can be compared. Yet the existence of a complete set of templates for all recognized stimuli seems implausible and their invocation does not appear to be part of a parsimonious solution to the problem. Quite the contrary, it is obviously a form of thinking engendered by the computer technology and programming arts of the 1950's, not by psychobiological evidence.

The assumption of a set of stored templates also leads to numerous other difficulties. It creates the further necessity of assuming the existence of an exhaustive comparison process to serve as the information-processing algorithm. As such, the template approach raises the need for a very high-speed computational system, which the brain certainly is not, as well as implying a requirement for a large and probably variable amount of time to carry out myriad comparisons. Obviously, this chain of logic, even in its simplest form, leads to a theoretical catastrophe; the template theory must be modified and remodified along lines that deviate considerably from the original premises of the simple, straightforward version and thereby lead to psychobiological absurdities. For example, the logistic difficulties that are immediately encountered in a template-matching, cross-correlational theory usually lead to discussions of associative memories and heuristic processing that go far afield from the geometry-dependent processes that are believed to underlie the kind of perception considered here. Clearly, there is considerable difficulty with the template-matching approach. However, if no templates are required and if some parallel algorithmic processing is substituted for a serial exhaustive searching process, a number of features of pattern recognition (such as comparable reaction times for patterns of comparable complexity and detectability, regardless of prior experience) immediately become realizable with models that are considerably more parsimonious.

At the very least, the elimination of the requirement for templates also mitigates the need to explain the ontogenetic or experiential development of a complete set of templates—a difficult task. Abandoning the template cross-correlational approach also reduces the need to explain how stimuli that have never been previously experienced or have never been seen in a particular orientation can be seen at all. The need for an escape hatch from cross-correlational processes seems clear indeed.

In sum, algorithmic (as opposed to exhaustive search) models, such as the autocorrelation model presented in this study, are parsimonious. Most of the information required to explain the particular detectability level of a given stimulus pattern is carried by the stimulus itself, and many different varieties of such information can be processed by a few relatively simple algorithmic mechanisms. Although the perceiver still resides in the observer, it is not necessary to assume that the neural information processor must change its nature with every change in stimulus configuration. What humans perceive remains very much a function of their nature, but differences in stimulus detectability can nevertheless be attributed to the intrinsic properties of the stimulus dimensions themselves.

Another general advantage of the autocorrelation process is that it is a plausible mechanism. The hypothetical neural network presented in Figure 3-18 invokes no unusual or exotic neural interconnections. Indeed, it requires no interactive processes other than simple spatial convergence and divergence; therefore, merely the simplest kind of spatial summative logical units are involved in the implementation of this algorithmic mechanism. No elaborate memorial units are needed, nor are any special and complex multiplexing circuits required to compare a stimulus with a large number of hypothetical stored templates. Although neural comparators must certainly exist at some other levels of the nervous system, this early stage of processing does not need them, and it is, therefore, conceptually no more complicated than the retinal plexus itself. Furthermore, it is a parallel processing network—a simplifying assumption that accelerates information processing and yet remains consistent with the known attributes of the neural networks in the visual system.

Another very important general advantage of the autocorrelation mechanism is its correspondence with what is known about visual perception. We have seen how the arrangement of the parts is more important than the nature of the parts in a prototypical pattern recognition task. Kolers' pictures of random stimuli, which we call "chairs," emphasize this point most effectively. The autocorrelation process is especially sensitive to the global geometry of the stimulus in a way that is almost unique among mathematical models of pattern recognition. All of these general comments suggest that a profound change in theoretical orientation must occur as the theoretician shifts his perspective away from theories that emphasize the recognition of specific parts (and their subsequent assembly into a global percept) to those that concentrate attention on the processing of the global arrangement itself.

In the context of the present study, more specifically, we have seen that the particular effects of a number of different parameters of stimulus shape and organization are modeled fairly well by this autocorrelation approach. The high degree of sensitivity to the periodic properties of the stimuli is a special strength of this model. It seems to be sensitive also to spacing, numerosity, and various other aspects of figural organization in much the same manner as that observed in the psychophysical data. However, it is insensitive to the orientation, displacement, and "goodness" (as metricized by Garner and Clement, 1963) in a way that is again consistent with the psychophysical findings.

Another general suggestion that emerges from the psychophysical data is that there may be a hierarchy of interactions between various

SUMMARY—AN ALTERNATIVE NEURAL IMPLEMENTATION 139

levels of the components of dotted figures. One form of interaction has been observed between the component dots of lines; the primitive parameters of spacing and numerosity have been influential factors affecting detectability. In addition, however, the global arrangement of the dots in the pattern can also affect its detectability. There appear to be several kinds of interactions, therefore, even among the individual dots of a pattern. Tests of polygonal detectability have suggested the existence of other echelons of interaction—ones in which the lines, themselves compound dot patterns, interact with each other, as lines, to influence the overall detectability of the forms. These interactions are influential even though the local geometry within the lines has been kept constant.

The findings of a hierarchy of interactions is another example of a major agreement between the psychophysical data and the autocorrelation model. Both the data and the model exhibit the same sensitivity to the same wide range of organizational parameters. Having all stages of this hierarchy of interactions modeled by a single mechanism—the autocorrelator—is a vigorous argument in support of the model's suitability as a descriptor of this type of pattern perception.

The autocorrelation model is a specific alternative to a model emphasizing highly specific feature-sensitive single neurons. The autocorrelation process is able to mimic a considerable amount of the psychophysical data obtained in this and related studies on the basis of information processing by a purely homogenous network of undifferentiated neurons. This is not to say that single cells, selectively responsive to various parameters of shape and time, are not to be found in the nervous system; Hubel and Wiesel's basic observations have been too often replicated to challenge their essential message. However, it may be appropriate to reexamine what these response categories mean. Instead of playing the role of the actual feature-filtering mechanisms of the form detection process itself, these single-cell responses may reflect the output of some other distributed network type of detection mechanism. They may be, in a certain sense, responders or effectors indicating the function of some more fundamental algorithmic processing mechanism, such as the autocorrelator proposed here.

Granted, this chain of reasoning is not compelling by itself. However, it is evident how the theoretical perspective drastically changes as the emphasis shifts from the one approach to the other—from a restrictive theory that concentrates on single cells as feature filters to one that encompasses the action of an ensemble of neurons acting as a collective parallel information processor in an algorithmic fashion as focused on in Pribram's (1969) analogy of the "holographic brain" or John's (1972) statistical theory of learning. (See also Pribram, Nuwer, & Baron, 1974).

This change in emphasis is an essential result of this study, for again, purely on intuitive and esthetic grounds, the difficulty of assigning priority to one neuron or type of neuron in a network made up of many millions is an inescapable concomitant of any theory based on the function of specialized single cells. However, even the simplest perceptual phenomena, all would agree, must be based on the concatenated action of many millions of neurons. A priori, network theories seem to be more authentic descriptions of what is going on in the brain than those based on single-cell functions.

This brings us to the final points of this study. The specific mathematical formularization presented here is, as has been noted, only one of many possible formulations that can satisfactorily model the form of perception tasks under consideration. Two other related facts are equally obvious.

First, this sort of mathematical exercise is a form of reasoning by analogy and it is highly unlikely that one or another theoretical approach will ever be conclusively established. Not only are there difficulties in establishing the exact neural process without direct examination (only the most preliminary steps have been taken by such workers as Pollen, Lee, & Taylor, 1971), but there are also formal similarities between the different theories that may make them equivalent in much the same way as the quantum and wave theories of electromagnetism are now thought to be—two different but equally "good" descriptions of the physical reality.

Second, it is probably true that the particular mathematics represented by each specific formulation reflects something more general than the particular aspect emphasized. For example, in the Fourier model, the notion of spatial frequencies is emphasized but, in fact, the basic theorem of Fourier analysis is that any wave form, no matter how complex, can be analyzed into a family of orthogonal components. Similarly, in autocorrelation models, the emphasis is directed

SUMMARY—AN ALTERNATIVE NEURAL IMPLEMENTATION 141

to a particular aspect of the form—its organization—but autocorrelation is also a general process particularly sensitive to periodicities. Therefore, both of these theories may work to a degree, by virtue of their generality, yet in doing so they may obscure some more fundamental aspect of the psychobiological computational process. In other words, the existence of a particular form of mathematics, originally developed to meet the needs of a considerably different physical system, does not necessarily mean that it is entirely suitable as a model of this brain process. What is needed more is a novel form of mathematics, especially designed for network interactions, that exhibits some of the properties of an autocorrelator but also exhibits some additional features that are likely to be found in the biological nerve net. The achievement of such a novel form of analysis is probably the only way we shall ever reach a perfect fit between the model and the psychophysical data.

What the present autocorrelation model does is to suggest a perspective alternative to those commonly accepted by contemporary psychobiologists. Furthermore, according to some criteria, it is more general than some of these other models, as well as being more parsimonious in the number of premises invoked.

These final comments present a picture of a theory that is not yet fully developed, that is not altogether unique, that is not precisely numerically predictive, and that is, sadly, probably unprovable physiologically. However, it must also be conceded that all other theories of pattern recognition share these limitations. Despite these constraints, the autocorrelation approach championed here does emphasize a particular point of view as to how these perceptual processes may be implemented in the neural substrate—a point of view that has much to support it in terms of the plausibility and the correspondence that exists between its predictions and human psychophysical data.

References

Allport, F. H. *Theories of perception and the concept of structure.* New York: Wiley, 1955.

Anderson, J. A. A memory storage model utilizing spatial correlation functions. *Kybernetik,* **5,** Heft 3, 1968, 113–119.

Anderson, J. A. Two models for memory organization using interacting traces. *Mathematical Biosciences,* 1970, **8,** 137–160.

Anderson, J. A. A simple neural network generating an interactive memory. *Mathematical Biosciences,* 1972, **14,** 197–200.

Anderson, J. A. A theory for the recognition of items from short memorized lists. *Psychological Review,* 1973, **80**(6), 417–438.

Andrews, D. P. Perception of contours in the central fovea. *Nature,* 1965, **205,** 1218–1220.

Appelle, S. Perception and discrimination as a function of stimulus orientation: The "oblique effect" in man and animals. *Psychological Bulletin,* 1972, **78,** 266–278.

REFERENCES

Attneave, F., & Arnoult, M. D. The quantitative study of shape and pattern perception. *Psychological Review*, 1956, **53**, 452–471.

Barlow, H. B., Fitzhugh, R., & Kuffler, S. W. Change of organization in the receptive fields of the cat's retina during dark adaptation. *Journal of Physiology*, 1957, **137**, 338–354.

Barlow, H. B. & Levick, W. R. The mechanism of directionally selective units in rabbit's retina. *Journal of Physiology*, 1965, **178**, 477–504.

Barlow, H. B., Narasimhan, R., & Rosenfeld, A. Visual pattern recognition in machines and animals. *Science*, 1972, **177**, 567–575.

Bell, H. H. & Lappin, J. S. Sufficient conditions for the discrimination of motion. *Perception & Psychophysics*, 1973, **14**, 45–50.

Bitterman, M. E., Krauskopf, J., & Hochberg, J. E. Threshold for visual form: A diffusion model. *American Journal of Psychology*, 1954, **67**, 205–219.

Blakemore, C., Nachmias, J., & Sutton, P. The perceived spatial frequency shift: Evidence for frequency-selective neurones in the human brain. *Journal of Physiology*, 1970, **210**, 727–750.

Blakemore, C. & Sutton, P. Size adaptation: A new aftereffect. *Science*, 1969, **166**, 245–247.

Blum, H. A transformation for extracting new descriptors of shape. In W. Wathen-Dunn (Ed.), *Models for the perception of speech and visual form*. Cambridge, Mass.: MIT Press, 1967. Pp. 362–380.

Brick, D. B. Pattern recognition, the challenge, are we meeting it? In S. Watanabe (Ed.), *Methodologies of pattern recognition*. New York: Academic Press, 1969. Pp. 75–96.

Brown, P. K., & Wald, G. Visual pigments in single rods and cones of the human retina: Direct measurements reveal mechanisms of human night and color vision. *Science*, 1964, **144**, 45–52.

Buchsbaum, W. H., & Mayzner, M. S. The effect of line length on sequential blanking. *Psychonomic Science*, 1969, **15**(2), 111–112.

Campbell, F. W., Cooper, G. F., & Enroth-Cugel, C. The spatial selectivity of the visual cells of the cat. *Journal of Physiology*, 1969, **203**, 223–235.

Campbell, F. W., Cooper, G. F., Robson, J. G., & Sachs, M. B. The spatial selectivity of visual cells of the cat and the squirrel monkey. *Journal of Physiology*, 1969, **204**, 120–121P.

Campbell, F. W., & Kulikowski, J. J. Orientational selectivity of the human visual system. *Journal of Physiology*, 1966, **187**, 437–445.

Campbell, F. W., Kulikowski, J. J., & Levinson, J. The effect of orientation on the visual resolution of gratings. *Journal of Physiology*, 1966, **187**, 427–436.

Campbell, F. W., & Maffei, L. Electrophysiological evidence for the existence of orientation and size detectors in the human visual system. *Journal of Physiology*, 1970, **207**, 635–652.

Campbell, F. W., Nachmias, J., & Jukes, J. Spatial-frequency discrimination in human vision. *Journal of the Optical Society of America*, 1970, **60**(4), 555–559.

REFERENCES

Campbell, F. W., & Robson, J. G. Application of Fourier analysis to the visibility of gratings. *Journal of Physiology,* 1968, **197,** 551–566.

Cherry, C. Two ears—but one world. In W. A. Rosenblith (Ed.), *Sensory communication: Contributions to the symposium on principles of sensory communication.* Cambridge, Mass.: MIT Press and New York: Wiley, 1961. Pp. 99–119.

Chinnis, J. O., Jr., & Uttal, W. R. Tachistoscopic detectability of dotted lines in dotted visual noise: The effect of the signal-to-noise ratio. *American Journal of Psychology,* 1975, in press.

Crook, M. N. Facsimile-generated analogues for instrumental forms displays. In J. W. Wulfeck & J. H. Taylor (Eds.), *Form discrimination as related to military problems.* Washington, D.C.: National Academy of Sciences–National Research Council, 1957. Pp. 85–98.

Dember, W. N., & Purcell, D. G. Recovery of masked visual targets by inhibition of the masking stimulus. *Science,* 1967, **157,** 1335–1336.

Deutsch, J. A. A theory of shape recognition. *British Journal of Psychology,* 1955, **46,** 30–37.

Dodwell, P. C. Shape recognition in rats. *British Journal of Psychology,* 1957, **48,** 221–229.

Dodwell, P. C. *Visual pattern recognition.* New York: Holt, Rinehart, and Winston, 1970.

Dodwell, P. C. On perceptual clarity. *Psychological Review,* 1971, **78,** 275–289.

Engel, G. R. The autocorrelation function and binocular brightness mixing. *Vision Research,* 1969, **9,** 1111–1130.

Engel, G. R., Dougherty, W. G., & Jones, G. B. Correlation and letter recognition. *Canadian Journal of Psychology,* 1973, **27,** 317–326.

Enroth-Cugel, C., & Robson, J. G. The contrast sensitivity of retinal ganglion cells of the cat. *Journal of Physiology,* 1966, **187,** 517–552.

Eriksen, C. W., & Collins, J. F. Sensory traces versus the psychological moment in the temporal organization of form. *Journal of Experimental Psychology,* 1968, **77**(3), 376–382.

Fitts, P. M., Weinstein, M., Rappaport, M., Anderson, N., & Leonard, J. A. Stimulus correlates of visual pattern recognition: A probability approach. *Journal of Experimental Psychology,* 1956, **51,** 1–11.

Fitzgerald, R. Unpublished doctoral dissertation, University of Western Australia, Nedlands, Western Australia, 1970.

Fox, S. S., & O'Brien, J. H. Duplication of evoked potential waveform by curve of probability of firing of a single cell. *Science,* 1965, **147,** 888–890.

French, R. S. Pattern recognition in the presence of visual noise. *Journal of Experimental Psychology,* 1954, **47,** 27–31.

Fry, G. A. Blur as a factor in form discrimination. In J. W. Wulfeck & J. H. Taylor (Eds.), *Form discrimination as related to military problems.* Washington, D.C.: National Academy of Sciences–National Research Council, 1957. Pp. 75–82.

REFERENCES

Garner, W. R. *Uncertainty and structure as psychological concepts.* New York: Wiley, 1962.

Garner, W. R. *The processing of information and structure.* Potomac, Md.: Lawrence Erlbaum Associates, 1974.

Garner, W. R., & Clement, D. E. Goodness of pattern and pattern uncertainty. *Journal of Verbal Learning & Verbal Behavior,* 1963, **2,** 446–452.

Gilinsky, A. S. Orientation-specific effects of patterns adapting light on visual acuity. *Journal of the Optical Society of America,* 1968, **58**(1), 13–18.

Glass, L. Moiré effect from random dots. *Nature,* 1969, **223,** 578–580.

Goble, L. Unpublished doctoral dissertation, University of Michigan, 1975.

Green, B. F. The use of high-speed digital computers in studies of form perception. In J. W. Wulfeck & J. H. Taylor (Eds.), *Form discrimination as related to military problems.* Washington, D.C.: National Academy of Sciences–National Research Council, 1957. Pp. 65–75.

Green, B. F. *Digital computers in research: An introduction for behavioral and social scientists.* New York: McGraw-Hill, 1963.

Grüsser, O.-J., & Klinke, R. (Eds.) *Pattern recognition in biological and technical systems.* Berlin: Springer-Verlag, 1971.

Haber, R. N., & Standing, L. G. Direct measures of short-term visual storage. *Quarterly Journal of Experimental Psychology,* 1969, **21**(1), 43–54.

Hartline, H. K., & Ratliff, F. Inhibitory interaction of receptor units in the eye of *Limulus. Journal of General Physiology,* 1957, **40**(3), 357–376.

Hartline, H. K., & Ratliff, F. Spatial summation of inhibitory influences in the eye of *Limulus,* and the mutual interaction of receptor units. *Journal of General Physiology,* 1958, **41,** 1049–1066.

Hartline, H. K., Wagner, H. G., & Ratliff, F. Inhibition in the eye of *Limulus. Journal of General Physiology,* 1956, **39**(5), 651–673.

Hebb, D. O. *Organization of behavior.* New York: Wiley, 1949.

Held, R. Two modes of processing spatially distributed visual stimulation. In F. O. Schmitt (Ed.), *The neurosciences: Second study program.* New York: Rockefeller University Press, 1970, Pp. 317–324.

Horwitz, L. P., & Shelton, G. L. Pattern recognition using autocorrelation. *Proceedings of the IRE,* 1961, **49,** 75–185.

Hubel, D. H., & Wiesel, T. N. Receptive fields, binocular interaction and functional architecture in the cat's visual cortex. *Journal of Physiology,* 1962, **160,** 106–154.

Hubel, D. H., & Wiesel, T. N. Shape and arrangement of columns in cat's striate cortex. *Journal of Physiology,* 1963, **165,** 559–568.

Hubel, D. H., & Wiesel, T. N. Receptive fields and functional architecture of monkey striate cortex. *Journal of Physiology,* 1968, **195,** 215–243.

John, E. R. Switchboard vs. statistical theories of learning and memory. *Science,* 1972, **177,** 850–864.

Julesz, B. *Foundations of cyclopean perception.* Chicago: University of Chicago Press, 1971.

Kabrisky, M. *A proposed model for visual information processing in the human brain.* Urbana, Ill.: University of Illinois Press, 1966.

Kahneman, D. Method, findings, and theory in studies of visual masking. *Psychological Bulletin,* 1968, **70**(6), 404–425.

Kinsbourne, M., & Warrington, E. K. The effect of an after-coming random pattern on the perception of brief visual stimuli. *Quarterly Journal of Experimental Psychology,* 1962, **14**(4), 223–234.

Kitterle, F. L. The possible locus of lightness contrast. *Perception & Psychophysics,* 1973, **14**, 585–589.

Köhler, W. *Gestalt psychology.* New York: Liveright, 1929.

Kolers, P. A. The role of shape and geometry in picture recognition. In B. S. Lipkin & A. Rosenfeld (Eds.), *Picture processing and psychopictorics.* New York: Academic Press, 1970. Pp. 181–202.

Kolers, P. A., & Perkins, D. N. Orientation of letters and errors in their recognition. *Perception & Psychophysics,* 1969, **5**(5), 265–269. (a)

Kolers, P. A., & Perkins, D. N. Orientation of letters and their speed of recognition. *Perception & Psychophysics,* 1969, **5**(5), 275–280. (b)

Kolers, P. A. & Rosner, B. S. On visual masking (metacontrast): Dichoptic observation. *American Journal of Psychology,* 1960, **73**, 1–21.

Kristofferson, A. B. Visual detection as influenced by target form. In J. W. Wulfeck & J. H. Taylor (Eds.), *Form discrimination as related to military problems.* Washington, D.C.: National Academy of Sciences–National Research Council, 1957.

Kristofferson, A. B., & Dember, W. N. Detectability of targets consisting of multiple small points of light. Report of Project Michigan, Vision Research Laboratories, The University of Michigan, September 1958.

Lashley, K. S. The problem of cerebral organization in vision. *Biological Symposia,* 1942, **7**, 301–322.

Lashley, K. S., Chow, K. L., & Semmes, J. An examination of the electrical field theory of cerebral integration. *Psychological Review,* 1951, **58**, 123–136.

Lendaris, G. G., & Stanley, G. L. Diffraction-pattern sampling for automatic pattern recognition. *Proceedings of the IEEE,* 1970, **58**, 198–216.

Lettvin, J. Y., Maturana, H. R., McCulloch, W. S., & Pitts, W. H. What the frog's eye tells the frog's brain. *Proceedings of the IRE,* 1959, **47**, 1940–1951.

Licklider, J. C. R. Three auditory theories. In S. Koch (Ed.), *Psychology: A study of a science. Study I. Conceptual and systematic. Volume I. Sensory, perceptual, and physiological formulations.* New York: McGraw-Hill, 1959. Pp. 41–144.

Maffei, L., Fiorentini, A., & Bisti, S. Neural correlate of perceptual adaptation to gratings. *Science,* 1973, **82**, 1036–1038.

Marks, W. B., Dobelle, W. H., & MacNichol, E. F., Jr. Visual pigments of single primate cones. *Science,* 1964, **143**(3611), 1181–1183.

Mayzner, M. S., & Tresselt, M. E. Visual information processing with sequential inputs: A general model for sequential blanking, displacement, and overprinting phenomena. *Annals of the New York Academy of Sciences,* 1970, **169**, 599–618.

Mayzner, M. S., Tresselt, M. E., & Helfer, M. S. A provisional model of visual information processing with sequential inputs. *Psychonomic Monograph Supplements,* 1967, **2**(7), 91–108.

McCullough, C. Color adaptation of edge-detectors in the human visual system. *Science,* 1965, **149**(3688), 1115–1116.

McLachlan, D., Jr. The role of optics in applying correlation functions to pattern recognition. *Journal of the Optical Society of America,* 1962, **52**, 454–459.

Meisel, W. S. *Computer-oriented approaches to pattern recognition.* Mathematics in Science and Engineering Series, Vol. 83. New York: Academic Press, 1972.

Meyer-Eppler, W. Die funktionalanalytische Behandlung des Schattenproblems. *Optik,* 1946, **1**, 465–474.

Meyer-Eppler, W., & Darius, G. Two-dimensional photographic autocorrelation of pictures and alphabet letters. In C. Cherry (Ed.), *Information theory.* New York: Academic Press, 1956. Pp. 34–36.

Minsky, M., & Papert, S. *Perceptrons: An introduction to computational geometry.* Cambridge, Mass.: MIT Press, 1969.

Montanari, U. On the optimal detection of curves in noisy pictures. *Communications of the AMC,* 1971, **14**(5), 335–345.

Nachmias, J. Effect of exposure duration on visual contrast sensitivity with square-wave gratings. *Journal of the Optical Society of America,* 1967, **57**, 421–427.

Neisser, U. *Cognitive psychology.* New York: Appleton Century Crofts, 1967.

Pastore, N. *Selective history of theories of visual perception 1650–1950.* London and New York: Oxford University Press, 1971.

Philips, W. R., & McLachlan, D., Jr. A versatile projector for assisting in crystal structure determinations. *Review of Scientific Instruments,* 1954, **25**, 123–128.

Pitts, W. H., & McCulloch, W. S. How we know universals: The perception of auditory and visual forms. *Bulletin of Mathematical Biophysics,* 1947, **9**, 127–147.

Platt, J. R. Functional geometry and the determination of pattern in mosaic receptors. In H. P. Yockey, R. L. Platzman, & H. Quastler (Eds.), *Symposium on information theory in biology.* New York: Pergamon Press, 1958. Pp. 371–398.

Platt, J. R. How a random array of cells can learn to tell whether a straight line is straight. In H. von Foerster & G. W. Zopf, Jr. (Eds.), *Principles of self-organization.* University of Illinois Symposium on Self-Organization—1961. New York: Pergamon Press, 1962. Pp. 315–321.

Pollen, D. A., Lee, J. R., & Taylor, J. H. How does the striate cortex begin the reconstruction of the visual world? *Science,* 1971, **173**, 74–77.

Prewitt, J. M. S. Object enhancement and extraction. In B. S. Lipkin & A. Rosenfeld (Eds.), *Picture processing and psychopictorics.* New York: Academic Press, 1970. Pp. 75–149.

REFERENCES

Pribram, K. H. The neurophysiology of remembering. *Scientific American,* 1969, **220**(1), 73–86.

Pribram, K. H., Nuwer, M., & Baron, R. The holographic hypothesis of memory structure in brain function and perception. In R. C. Atkinson, D. H. Krantz, R. C. Luce, & P. Suppes (Eds.), *Contemporary developments in mathematical psychology,* Vol. II. San Francisco: Freeman, 1974.

Ratliff, F. *Mach bands: Quantitative studies on neutral networks in the retina.* San Francisco: Holden Day, 1965.

Reichardt, W. Autocorrelation, a principle for the evaluation of sensory information by the central nervous system. In W. A. Rosenblith (Ed.), *Sensory communication: Contributions to the symposium on principles of sensory communication.* Cambridge, Mass.: MIT Press and New York: John Wiley, 1961. Pp. 303–317.

Rosenblatt, F. The perceptron: A probabilistic model for information storage and organization in the brain. *Psychological Review,* 1958, **65**, 386–408.

Rosenfeld, A., Thomas, R. B., & Lee, Y. H. Edge and curve enhancement in digital pictures. Technical Report 69-93, Computer Science Center, University of Maryland, College Park, Maryland, 1969.

Ross, J. and Hogben, J. H. A short-term memory in stereopsis. *Vision Research,* 1974, **14**, 1195–1201.

Rothberg, J. M. Simulation of neural nets with some applications to visual information processing. *Computers & Biomedical Research,* 1968, **1**, 435–451.

Sachs, M. B., Nachmias, J., & Robson, J. G. Spatial-frequency channels in human vision. *Journal of the Optical Society of America,* 1971, **61**(9), 1176–1186.

Schiller, P. H. Monoptic and dichoptic visual masking by patterns and flashes. *Journal of Experimental Psychology,* 1965, **69**(2), 193–199.

Schiller, P. H. Forward and backward masking as a function of relative overlap and intensity of test and masking stimuli. *Perception & Psychophysics,* 1966, **1**, 161–164.

Schiller, P. H. Single unit analysis of backward visual masking and metacontrast in the cat lateral geniculate nucleus. *Vision Research,* 1968, **8**, 855–866.

Schiller, P. H. Behavioral and electrophysiological studies of visual masking. In K. N. Leibovic (Ed.), *Information processing in the nervous system.* New York: Springer-Verlag, 1969. Pp. 141–165.

Selfridge, O. G. Pandemonium: A paradigm for learning. In *The mechanization of thought processes: A Symposium.* London: H.M. Stationery Office, 1959.

Simmons, J. A. Echolocation in bats: Signal processing of echoes for target range. *Science,* 1971, **171**, 925–928.

Sperling, G. A model for visual memory tasks. *Human Factors,* 1963, **5**, 19–31.

Sperry, R. W., Miner, N., & Myers, R. E. Visual pattern perception following subplial slicing and tantalum wire implantations in the visual cortex. *Journal of Comparative & Physiological Psychology,* 1955, **48**, 50–58.

Sutherland, N. S. Visual discrimination of orientation and shape by the octopus. *Nature,* 1957, **179,** 11–13.

Sutherland, N. S. Comments on the session. In W. Wathen-Dunn (Ed.), *Models for the perception of speech and visual form.* Cambridge, Mass.: MIT Press, 1967. Pp. 239–243.

Turvey, M. T. On peripheral and central processes in vision: Inferences from an information-processing analysis of masking with patterned stimuli. *Psychological Review,* 1973, **80**(1), 1–52.

Uhr, L. (Ed.) *Pattern recognition: Theory, experiment, computer simulations, and dynamic models of form perception and discovery.* New York: Wiley, 1966.

Uhr, L., & Vossler, C. A pattern-recognition program that generates, evaluates, and adjusts its own operators. In E. Feigenbaum & J. Feldman (Eds.), *Computers and thought.* New York: McGraw-Hill, 1963. Pp. 251–268.

Uttal, W. R. Masking of alphabetic character recognition by dynamic visual noise (DVN). *Perception & Psychophysics,* 1969, **6**(2), 121–128.

Uttal, W. R. On the physiological basis of masking with dotted visual noise. *Perception & Psychophysics,* 1970, **7**(6), 321–327.

Uttal, W. R. A masking approach to the problem of form perception. *Perception & Psychophysics,* 1971, **9**(3A), 296–298.

Uttal, W. R. A minor perturbing effect of retinal locus on dot pattern recognition: Rejection of a possible artifact. *Psychonomic Science,* 1972, **29**(2), 100–102.

Uttal, W. R. *The psychobiology of sensory coding.* New York: Harper & Row, 1973. (a)

Uttal, W. R. The effect of deviations from linearity on the detection of dotted line patterns. *Vision Research,* 1973, **13,** 2155–2163. (b)

Uttal, W. R., Bunnell, L. M., & Corwin, S. On the detectability of straight lines in visual noise: An extension of French's paradigm into the millisecond domain. *Perception & Psychophysics,* 1970, **8**(6), 385–388.

von Békésy, G. Mach- and Hering-type lateral inhibition in vision. *Vision Research,* 1968, **8,** 1483–1499.

Watanabe, S. (Ed.) *Methodologies of pattern recognition.* New York: Academic Press, 1969.

Wathen-Dunn, W. (Ed.) *Models for the perception of speech and visual form.* Cambridge, Mass.: MIT Press, 1967.

Weintraub, D. J., & Krantz, D. H. The Poggendorf illusion: Amputations, rotations, and other perturbations. *Perception & Psychophysics,* 1971, **10,** 257–264.

Weisstein, N. Backward masking and models of perceptual processing. *Journal of Experimental Psychology,* 1966, **72,** 232–240.

Weisstein, N. A Rashevsky–Landahl neural net: Stimulation of metacontrast. *Psychological Review,* 1968, **75,** 494–521.

Weisstein, N. What the frog's eye tells the human brain: Single cell analyzers in the human visual system. *Psychological Bulletin,* 1969, **72,** 157–176.

Weisstein, N., & Bisaha, J. Gratings mask bars and bars mask gratings: Visual frequency response to aperiodic stimuli. *Science,* 1972, **176,** 1047–1049.

Weisz, A. The use of facsimile equipment and controlled visual noise in forms research. In J. W. Wulfeck & J. H. Taylor (Eds.), *Form discrimination as related to military problems.* Washington, D.C.: National Academy of Sciences–National Research Council, 1957. Pp. 83–84.

Whitfield, I. C., & Evans, E. F. Responses of auditory cortical neurons to stimuli of changing frequency. *Journal of Neurophysiology* 1965, **28,** 655–672.

Williamson, H. Algorithm 420: Hidden-line plotting program [J6]. *Communication of the ACM,* 1972, **15**(2), 100–103.

Wulfeck, J. W., & Taylor, J. H. (Eds.) *Form discrimination as related to military problems.* Washington, D.C.: National Academy of Sciences–National Research Council, 1957.

Zusne, L. *Visual perception of form.* New York: Academic Press, 1970.

Author Index

Numbers in *italics* refer to the pages on which the complete references are listed.

A

Allport, F. H., 12, *142*
Anderson, J. A., 27, 28, *142*
Anderson, N., 36, *144*
Andrews, D. P., 18, *142*
Appelle, S., 43, *142*
Attneave, F., 2, *143*
Arnoult, M. D., 2, *143*

B

Barlow, H. B., 15, 17, 20, 22, 39, 132, *143*
Baron, R., 140, *148*
Bell, H. H., 24, *143*
Bisaha, J., 25, *150*
Bisti, S., 132, *146*
Bitterman, M. E., 15, *143*
Blakemore, C., 18, 25, *143*
Blum, H., 15, *143*
Brick, D. B., 23, *143*
Brown, P. K., 135, *143*
Buchsbaum, W. H., 18, *143*
Bunnell, L. M., 9, 40, 47, 106, *149*

AUTHOR INDEX

C

Campbell, F. W., 18, 25, 44, *143, 144*
Cherry, C., 27, *144*
Chinnis, J. O., Jr., 40, 52, 54, 55, *144*
Chow, K. L., 14, *146*
Clement, D. E., 9, 36, 47, 66, 78, 118, 123, 138, *146*
Collins, J. F., 36, 37, *144*
Cooper, G. F., 25, *143*
Corwin, S., 9, 40, 47, 106, *149*
Crook, M. N., 36, *144*

D

Darius, G., 96, *147*
Dember, W. N., 6, 18, *144, 146*
Deutsch, J. A., 19, *144*
Dobelle, W. H., 135, *146*
Dodwell, P. C., 10, 12, 19, 28, 93, *144*
Dougherty, W. G., 27, *144*

E

Engel, G. R., 27, 93, *144*
Enroth-Cugel, C., 25, *143, 144*
Eriksen, C. W., 36, 37, *144*
Evans, E. F., 132, *150*

F

Fiorentini, A., 132, *146*
Fitts, P. M., 36, *144*
Fitzgerald, R., 37, *144*
Fitzhugh, R., 39, *143*
Fox, S. S., 14, *144*
French, R. S., 36, *144*
Fry, G. A., 36, *144*

G

Garner, W. R., 9, 36, 47, 66, 78, 80, 118, 123, 138, *145*
Gilinsky, A. S., 25, *145*
Glass, L., 28, *145*
Goble, L., 25, *145*
Green, B. F., 7, 36, *145*
Grüsser, O.-J., 12, *145*

H

Haber, R. N., 37, *145*
Hartline, H. K., 15, *145*
Hebb, D. O., 12, *145*
Held, R., 38, *145*
Helfer, M. S., 18, *147*
Hochberg, J. E., 15, *143*
Hogben, J. H., 36, *148*
Horwitz, L. P., 28, *145*
Hubel, D. H., 15, 19, 132, *145*

J

John, E. R., 140, *145*
Jones, G. B., 27, *144*
Jukes, J., 25, *143*
Julesz, B., 24, 36, *145*

K

Kabrisky, M., 24, *145*
Kahneman, D., 37, *146*
Kinsbourne, M., 37, 88, *146*
Kitterle, F. L., 43, *146*
Klinke, R., 12, *145*
Köhler, W., 14, *146*
Kolers, P. A., 3, 4, 43, 82, *146*
Krantz, D. H., 43, *149*
Krauskopf, J., 15, *143*
Kristofferson, A. B., 6, *146*
Kuffler, S. W., 39, *143*
Kulikowski, J. J., 18, 44, *143*

L

Lappin, J. S., 24, *143*
Lashley, K. S., 14, 25, *146*
Lee, J. R., 25, 132, 140, *147*
Lee, Y. H., 22, *148*
Lendaris, G. G., 25, *146*
Leonard, J. A., 36, *144*
Levick, W. R., 20, 132, *143*
Levinson, J., 44, *143*
Lettvin, J. Y., 15, 132, *146*
Licklider, J. C. R., 27, *146*

M

MacNichol, E. F., Jr., 135, *146*
Maffei, L., 25, 132, *143, 146*
Marks, W. B., 135, *146*
Maturana, H. R., 15, 132, *146*
Mayzner, M. S., 18, *143, 146, 147*
McCulloch, W. S., 15, 19, 132, *146, 147*
McCullough, C., 18, *147*

AUTHOR INDEX

McLachlan, D., Jr., 96, *147*
Meisel, W. S., 23, *147*
Meyer-Eppler, W., 96, *147*
Miner, N., 14, *148*
Minsky, M., 21, *147*
Montanari, U., 22, *147*
Myers, R. E., 14, *148*

N

Nachmias, J., 25, 39, *143, 147, 148*
Narasimhan, R., 15, 17, 22, *143*
Neisser, U., 12, *147*
Nuwer, M., 140, *148*

O

O'Brien, J. H., 14, *144*

P

Papert, S., 21, *147*
Pastore, N., 12, *147*
Perkins, D. N., 43, *146*
Philips, W. R., 96, *147*
Pitts, W. H., 15, 19, 132, *146, 147*
Platt, J. R., 13, *147*
Pollen, D. A., 24, 132, 140, *147*
Prewitt, J. M. S., 26, *147*
Pribram, K. H., 140, *148*
Purcell, D. G., 18, *144*

R

Rappaport, M., 36, *144*
Ratliff, F., 7, 15, *145, 148*
Reichardt, W., 27, *148*
Robson, J. G., 25, *143, 144, 148*
Rosenblatt, F., 21, *148*
Rosenfeld, A., 15, 17, 22, *143, 148*
Rosner, B. S., 82, *146*
Ross, J., 36, *148*
Rothberg, J. M., 19, *148*

S

Sachs, M. B., 25, *143, 148*
Schiller, P. H., 37, 81, 82, *148*
Selfridge, O. G., 21, *148*

Semmes, J., 14, *146*
Shelton, G. L., 28, *145*
Simmons, J. A., 24, *148*
Sperling, G., 86, *148*
Sperry, R. W., 14, *148*
Standing, L. G., 37, *145*
Stanley, G. L., 25, *146*
Sutherland, N. S., 2, 19, *149*
Sutton, P., 18, 25, *143*

T

Taylor, J. H., 25, 36, 132, 140, *147, 150*
Thomas, R. B., 22, *148*
Tresselt, M. E., 18, *146, 147*
Turvey, M. T., 5, 37, 82, 87, 91, *149*

U

Uhr, L., 12, 22, *149*
Uttal, W. R., 7, 8, 9, 19, 37, 38, 40, 46, 47, 49, 50, 52, 54, 55, 58, 81, 103, 106, 108, 124, *144, 149*

V

von Békésy, G., 6, 36, 38, *149*
Vossler, C., 22, *149*

W

Wagner, H. G., 15, *145*
Wald, G., 135, *143*
Warrington, E. K., 37, 88, *146*
Watanabe, S., 12, 23, *149*
Wathen-Dunn, W., 2, 12, *149*
Weinstein, M., 36, *144*
Weintraub, D. J., 43, *149*
Weisstein, N., 18, 19, 25, *149, 150*
Weisz, A., 36, *150*
Whitfield, I. C., 132, *150*
Wiesel, T. N., 15, 19, 132, *145*
Williamson, H., 98, *150*
Wulfeck, J. W., 36, *150*

Z

Zusne, L., 2, 12, *150*

Subject Index

A

Acuity threshold, 5
Adaptive automata, 21
Algorithm, 134, 140
Algorithmic models, 137
Algorithmic processing, 92
Alphabetic characters, 47
Amplitude
  differences of, 95
  enhancement of, 101
Angles, 46, 90, 106, 108
Anisotropic metric, 134
Aperiodic components, 26
Apparatus, 32
Arrangement, 37

Artificial intelligence, 20
Association units, 21
Autocorrelation, 11, 23, 25, 26, 28, 30, 133
  function, 95, 127
  hypothesis, 131
  model, 27, 52, 93, 96, 112
  one-dimensional, 27, 94
  theory, 94
  transform, 55, 93, 95, 100
  two-dimensional, 26, 94
  value C_a, 98
Autocorrelator
  digital, 28
  optical, 28
  spatial neural, 136

SUBJECT INDEX 155

Autocorrelogram, 98, 99, 101, 103, 104, 108
   peaks in, 99
      interaction among, 100
Averaging, 26

B

Backward masking, 83, 88, 91
Bar patterns, 44
Bat's echo ranging, 24
Bessel functions, 26
Binaural fusion, 27
Binocular luminance, 27
Black box, 20
Blur, 39
Boundary conditions, 9
Bright flash, 37, 82
Brightness, 39, 68
   differences in, 103
   inhibition of, 88

C

Caricature, 92
Cartesian coordinate system, 134
Cell assemblies, 13
Central decision processor, 87
Central locus, 82
Central nervous system, 85
Character recognition, 28
Chebyshev polynomials, 26
Chromatic threshold, 5
Cognitive functions, 131
Cognitive information processing, 8
Coherent light, 25
Collinearity, 52, 53, 56, 90, 109
Color
   adaptation, 18
   effects, 132
   vision, 135
Combination tones, 27
Complex cells, 30
Component parts, 77
Compound evoked potentials, 14
Computational algorithms, 23
Computational network, 20, 21, 132
Computer, 32, 97
Computer simulation, 129
Constant cortical spacing, 134
Contour-sensitive systems, 38
Contrast of gratings, 132

Convergent summation, 129
Correlation theories, 23, 24, 29
Cortical network, 130
Cross correlation, 23, 24, 92, 134
Curvature, 46, 47, 90, 106, 108

D

d', 40
Data processing procedures
   parallel, 95
   serial, 95
Decision algorithms, 23
Δx, Δy space, 101
Detection, 7, 40
Diagonals, 79
Dichoptic presentation, 85
Direct proof, 135
Direction sensitivity, 18, 20
Discrepancies, 122, 126
Discrete network interactions, 29
Disorganization, 91
Displacement, 138
Dots, 32, 39
   distance between, 90
   luminosity, 35
   masking, 35, 39, 81, 82, 123
   mixing experiments, 28
   numerosity, 40, 43, 54, 104, 139
   ordered array of, 10
   patterns, 2, 7, 8, 39, 65, 78, 133
   spacing, 9, 40, 52, 100, 104, 108, 109
Dotted noise, 100
Dotted stimuli, 36
Dotted triangles, 90
Dotted visual noise, 40
Duration of exposure, 39
Dynamic noise, 59

E

Edge detectors, 18
Electronic spread, 14
Encoding, 8
Ensemble of neurons, 140
Equivalence, 133
Excitatory inputs, 128
Eye movements, 12, 13

F

Feature detection, 26, 30
Feature filter, 13, 26, 92, 134

SUBJECT INDEX

Feature-sensitive neurons, 95, 96, 139
Feedback signal, 35, 84
Field effects, 14
Fields of electrical activity, 13
Figural goodness, 36, 47, 65, 78, 80, 91, 118, 122
Figural organization, 66, 69, 74
Figure of merit, 99, 100, 104, 129, 133
Firing frequency, 129
Form, 1, 2
Form detection, 10, 139
Forward masking, 91
   binocular, 83
   dichoptic, 82, 83
   monoptic, 83
Fourier analysis, 24, 25, 132
Fourier transform, 11, 23, 133
Fourier-like spatial frequency specificity, 96

G

Geometry, 7, 35, 47, 100, 114, 135
Gestalt, 22
   psychologists, 65, 78
   school of psychology, 13
   terms, 66
   theory, 10
Global algorithms, 22
Global brain state, 129
Global density, 132
Global forms, 2, 22, 74
Global geometry, 61
Global organization, 11, 61
Global pattern, 48, 65, 132
"Goodness," 78, 80, 118, 138
Good organization, 69
Grid adaptation, 132
Grid density, 104
Group properties, 11

H

Hering type of inhibition, 38
Hermann grid, 6, 7
Hidden part, 98
Hierarchy of cells, 19
Hierarchy of interactions, 139
High-speed printer, 98
Histograms, 36

Holographic brain, 140
Homogenous sheets, 30, 95

I

Icon, 86
Identification task, 40
Image processing, 25
Image transformation, 23
Index of deviation, 57
Individual neurons, 131
Information, 60, 100
Information-processing models, 134
Inhibition
   Mach type, 38
   Hering type, 38
Inhibitory interaction, 20
Input–output analysis, 134
Integrals, 127
Integration, 129
Interaction
   between dots, 90
   between lines, 139
   echelons of, 139
   process of, 72
Irregular spacing, 52, 56
Irregularity, 54, 109
Isomorphism, 103, 127, 128, 136
Isotropic sheet of neurons, 26

L

Laser, 44
Lateral conducting connectives, 7, 127
Lateral inhibitory interaction, 18, 19, 38
Lateral interaction, 10
Law of Pragnanz, 66
Leading mask, 87
Letters, masking of, 81
Local geometry, 68
Logarithmic steps, 134
Logical networks, 14
Luminous threshold, 5, 6, 7

M

Mach band, 6, 7
Magnification, 91
Masking, 7, 8, 10, 32, 79, 88
Mathematical formularizations, 133
Matrix, 96, 126
Medial axis function (MAF), 15

SUBJECT INDEX

Memorial units, 138
Memory, 27
Metacontrast paradigm, 37
Microbits, 129
Microspectrophotometrics, 135
Microstructure, 117
Misregistration, 84
Molar psychological bits, 129
Motor response, 12
Multidimensional information processing, 80
Multilevel models of visual perception, 5
Multiple-cell theory, 92
Multiple-dot patterns, 6
Multipliers, 128

N

Neural comparators, 138
Neural intensity dimension, 103
Neural interconnection, 127
Neural levels, 39
Neural multipliers, 129
Neural network, 19, 126, 127, 131, 135, 137
Neural representation, 8
Neurophysiological theories, 13, 14
Nonlocal properties, 22

O

Optical analog computer, 96
Optical diffraction patterns, 25
Optical Fourier analysis, 24
Optomotor responses, 27
Organization, 37, 65, 73, 77, 80, 91, 100, 112, 139
Orientation, 43, 44, 62, 65, 90, 138
Oscilloscope, 96, 98

P

Parallel communication lines, 39
Parallel formations, 69
Parallelograms, 66, 68, 74, 90, 112
Parallel processing, 12, 95, 100, 129, 134, 138, 140
Pandemonium model, 21
Perceptron, 21
Perceptual development, 21
Perceptual contour enhancement effects, 6

Perceptual contour enhancement effects (*contd.*)
   Mach band, 6
   Hermann grid, 6
Periodic impulse, 26
Periodic properties, 95, 129
Periodic stimulus, 26
Peripheral masking model, 88
Phase sequence, 13
Phosphor P-15, 32
Photopigments, 135
Pick-up sticks, 69, 114
Pictographic mappings, 92
Picture-processing algorithm, 22
Place theories, 27
Poggendorf illusion, 43
Polar coordinate, 134
Polygonal geometry, 65
Polygonal rotation, 70
Polygons, 62, 90, 109, 139
Power spectrum density, 11, 23, 133
Procedure, 34
Pythagorean correction factor, 108
Pythagorean distance, 100, 126

Q

Quasi-periodic time series, 27
Quasi-random patterns, 69
Quantum mechanics, 114

R

R, 53
Radar tracking performance, 36
Random forms, 2
Random net, 21
Random pattern, 2
Random spacing, 53
Random visual noise, 59
Reaction times, 80
Receptor units, 21
Recognition criteria, 92
Redundancy, 66, 112
Replicas, 94, 127, 128
Response units, 21
Retinal plexus, 138
Rotation, 124

S

Secondary discrepancies, 117
Self-congruence, 13
Self-masking, 84

Sensory–motor theories, 12, 29
Sequential blanking, 18
Sequential stimulation, 38
Serial data processing procedures, 95
Shape, 139
Shift and compare, 94
Shifted replicas, 127
Signal extraction, 7, 101
Signal-to-noise ratios, 36
Silhouette, 92
Simple cells, 19, 30
Simulation model, 96
Simultaneous brightness contrast effect, 43
Single-cell neurophysiological theories, 15, 92
Space shifts, 94
Spacing, 139
Spatial convergence, 137
Spatial divergence, 137
Spatial frequency, 132, 133
Spatial illusions, 132
Spatial interaction, 6
Spatial summative logical units, 138
Specification of categories, 9
Spectral absorption fundamentals, 135
Spike action potential, 129
Squares, 74, 83, 90
　corners of, 118
　pattern, 76
Stage 3
　function, 89
　process, 136
Staircase order, 77
Statistical theory of learning, 140
Stereopsis, 36
Stimulus
　features, 29
　organization, 138
　shape, 138
Straight line, 1, 52, 90
Subjects, 31
Summatory interaction, 20
Symbolic encoding, 136

T

Tachistoscopic exposure, 13
Target detection, 36
Template, 24, 92, 132, 134
　model, 24, 52
　theory, 136
Temporal overlap, 86
Time, 139
Time delays, 94
Topologically constant, 8, 127
Topologically isomorphic, 130
Transform, 26, 101
Transform space, 99
Translation, 91, 124, 126
Transverse, 56
Transverse displacement, 56
Triangle, 59, 69, 74, 83, 90, 109, 118
　corners, 60, 62, 74, 112, 118
　critical parts in, 58
　patterns, 126
　sides, 60, 112
Trigger features, 15, 18, 132
Two-alternative forced-choice design, 34
Typed alphabetic characters, 43

U

Unit shifts, 26

V

Visual field, 127
Visual noise, 32, 35, 133
Visual processing
　Stage 1, 5
　Stage 2, 6
　Stage 3, 7
　Stage 4, 8
　Stages 5 and 6, 9
Voluntary eye movement, 12

W

Wave and quantum controversy, 11

LIBRARY OF DAVIDSON COLLEGE

Books on regular loan may be checked out for **two weeks**. Books must be presented at the Circulation Desk in order to be renewed.

A fine is charged after date due.

Special books are subject to special regulations at the discretion of library staff.

JAN -4 '82